Chess Players' Thinking

Chess has always been of interest to cognitive psychologists because it provides a way of investigating processes like thinking, memory, problem solving and the differences between machine and human processes. *Chess Players' Thinking* presents a new view about experts' thinking and how it should be studied. It provides a comprehensive analysis of chess players' cognition, but its main results should be generalizable to broader research on human expertise.

Chess Players' Thinking provides readers interested in human cognitive skills with a new concept-based approach. It introduces and reanalyses a number of classic psychological concepts such as apperception and restructuring. It will be of great interest to all cognitive psychologists and scientists working on human skills.

Pertti Saariluoma is based in the Department of Psychology at the University of Helsinki. He is a Senior Fellow in the Academy of Finland.

Chess Players' Thinking

A cognitive psychological approach

Pertti Saariluoma

London and New York

First published 1995
by Routledge
11 New Fetter Lane, London EC4P 4EE

Simultaneously published in the USA and Canada
by Routledge
29 West 35th Street, New York, NY 10001

© 1995 Pertti Saariluoma

Typeset in Times by J&L Composition Ltd, Filey, North Yorkshire
Printed and bound in Great Britain by
Biddles Ltd, Guildford and King's Lynn

British Cataloguing in Publication Data
A catalogue record for this book is available from the British Library

Library of Congress Cataloguing in Publication Data
A catalogue record for this book has been requested

ISBN 0–415–12079–9

Contents

Illustrations

FIGURES

TABLE

Preface

Chess players' thinking is a problem with an important position within the cognitive psychology of thinking. The work of Alfred Binet, Adriaan de Groot, Herbert Simon and a number of other researchers has made this task environment a generally acknowledged field in expertise research. The research into chess players' thinking has led to a number of important theoretical contributions that have laid down the foundations of the modern psychology of cognitive expertise. Consequently, it can be expected that any essential improvement in understanding chess players' thinking should also enrich our knowledge of cognitive expertise in general.

Chess and chess players' thinking are combinations of simplicity and complexity. Perhaps this is the ultimate reason why chess research has been so successful in pioneering research. The elements of chess comprise only thirty-two pieces on sixty-four squares. Yet the combinatorial possibilities have made it impossible for any current computer or the millions of chess enthusiasts to find a 'solution' to this game; that is, whether the game should result in a win for White, a win for Black or a draw, given best play on both sides. This combination of apparent simplicity and ultimate complexity has proven to be very helpful in psychological research. The simplicity makes it easy to investigate experimentally, and the complexity provides ecologically valid thinking processes for research.

In this book I try to make use of the experimentally tractable and cognitively rich nature of chess to consider theoretical issues. The book is not a textbook of chess research but a discourse on a number of theoretical and metatheoretical principles of problem-solving research in the context of chess players' thinking. At the same time I also try to show that critiques which target complex problem-solving research can be met by conceptual analysis and by refining the conceptual systems.

Conceptual analysis is a non-standard idea in empirical psychology. According to the standard view researchers derive hypotheses from the existing theories and test them empirically. If the outcome of the experiment falsifies the hypothesis, the theory is modified. In this way psychological knowledge grows through hypothesis testing and falsification. This 'official' view is oversimplified, because it underrates the significance of theoretical concepts and of theory-ladenness of facts in scientific development.

In practice, the theoretical notions of complex problem-solving research such as problem space have not been derived by testing empirical predictions from the once prevalent behaviourist and Gestalt theoretical models. Problem space is an ingenious conceptual innovation, and is based on conceptual considerations. Of course, it may have been inspired by the needs of simulation, for example, but it has not been found by the empirical testing of old theories. This is why we should not overstate the significance of theory testing and underestimate the role of theoretical concepts in the progress of cognitive psychology. When empirical observations provide us with answers the theoretical concepts form the limits for our questions, and the questions are as important as the answers for the ultimate success of the scientific endeavour.

Despite the incontrovertible importance of theoretical concepts psychologists have been seriously interested in the conceptual systems only during the major theoretical crises. The behaviourist and cognitive revolutions are examples of periods of rapid conceptual development. However, during the times between the revolutions conceptual development has led a silent life. At these times much more attention has been given to empirical facts than to theoretical and conceptual analyses. At the worst, it has been practically taboo to doubt the rationality of the established conceptual system.

The standard practice has led to an uneven development in psychology, characterized by an uncontrolled alternation between the periods of theoretical revolution and theoretical stagnation. Since the alternation seems to concentrate around concepts, it is rational to develop methods for continuous conceptual reflection. The main metatheoretical goal of this book is to improve conceptual analysis.

When beginning my work on chess players' thinking in 1976, I was originally interested in one concept, namely selectivity in thinking. Hardly anyone can deny the relevance of selectivity as an attribute of human thinking, but even now the notion of selective thinking itself has not received much attention in theoretical discussions. The notion is taken intuitively without any deeper reflection, and hence we have not been able to understand much about the mechanisms behind the selectivity leading to the economy of human thinking.

Not surprisingly, one can find two unrelated concepts of selectivity in the literature on chess players' thinking, which can be characterized as capacity oriented and content specific. Linked to the former is the kind of information selection which arises from the well-known limits of the human information processing system. The latter notion refers to the form of information selection which is based on the semantic contents of the representational elements. The main focus of attention over the years has been directed towards capacity-oriented information selection. Despite being widely used in expertise research, there is a much poorer understanding of the concept of semantically based information selection.

The typical approach to content-specific selectivity involves rather formal concepts. The standard notions such as stimulus equivalence, fixation, set, einstellung, affordances, top-down v. bottom-up processes, heuristics, schema, plans, pattern recognition, productions, scripts, 'seeing', etc. are simply too narrow and specific to express all aspects of selection of the information content of representations. They lack expressive power, when we try to consider all aspects of economical information processing, and they impose unnecessary conceptual limitations on theoretical work.

In contrast, the notions of fixation, set and einstellung refer to the behaviour of the subjects rather than their internal representations. Heuristics provide only probabilistic descriptions of information selection. Productions, pattern recognition, plans and schemata express how learned knowledge is applied but provide scant basis for describing the creative dynamics of representing. In addition they are not applicable over the whole field of thought research. Plans, for example, have very little relevance in the decision-making or categorization literature. Finally, the classic chess psychological term 'seeing' ignores the fact that the information content of representations need not be directly related to the physical stimulus.

Being dissatisfied with the conceptual intuitions behind the current terminology I have searched for an intuitively more precise and general concept for describing the content-specific mechanisms behind the construction of mental representations in chess. For these reasons I have reintroduced the old concept and theoretical problem of apperception. This notion, which was formulated by some of the brightest brains in the history of human learning, such as Leibniz and Kant, seems to have quite surprising expressive power. Defined as the process of content-specific mental representation construction, which is very precisely what the great philosophers in their time meant, in a simple way it opens numerous conceptual possibilities for study as to why some mental contents belong together in representations and why some other, equally plausible-looking combinations of elements are senseless. The basic question of apperception research is then why the human mind is able to construct economical representations, and what are the cognitive mechanisms that free the contents of mind from the slavery of the immediately given perceptual information and give the representations a non-stimulus bound, self-consistent and highly purposeful character.

In the first chapter, the problems of conceptual analysis are introduced. This chapter shows how current practice has almost totally overlooked the importance of theoretical concepts. The second chapter is preparatory and presents the task environment and the main theories in the field. In the third chapter attentional processes are considered and in the fourth memory is the main topic. The research into chess players' memory and attention has been very capacity oriented. These two chapters summarize the knowledge we have about the cognitive capacity of chess players.

The fifth chapter begins the content-specific analysis of thought. In it a new theoretical concept, apperception, is introduced. It will be shown how mind can very economically construct task-specific representations and how a small number of content-specific principles can explain the economical nature of the representations. This is empirically one of the core points of the book, because it shows that the economy of human thought compared to that of computers can perfectly well be explained by a small set of content-specific principles without assuming any probabilistic notions such as heuristics.

The sixth chapter concentrates on dynamics of thought and discusses restructuring. This process is needed in breaking the apperceived structures to make room for alternation of hypothetical representations, which is very characteristic of the human mind. The final chapter collects the main lines of the arguments and poses them in a wider frame of reference. Of particular interest will be the inability of capacity to explain the content-specific aspects of thought.

Indeed, the difference between capacity and contents seems to entail one of the deepest chasms in the world of learning. While capacity belongs to the sphere of causalistic natural sciences, the contents of thought seems to be an issue of functional humanistic research. But this is not really incomprehensible. If we think Man made world, it is functional to the minutest detail. It is functional because it is a product of human thought and this is the reason why the contents of human thought should be approached functionally as has been done in this book.

Acknowledgements

The basic ideas of this book have developed slowly over a period of a decade. It has been affected by personal contacts to a number of eminent cognitive psychologists. Especially, I should mention Alan Allport, who was, to my knowledge, the first to formulate precisely the difference between capacity and contents; Herbert Simon, whose theory of chess players' problem solving is the ground on which many of the current ideas have been built; and Alan Baddeley, whose research on working memory has inspired over many years my attempts to understand the operation of chess players' memory.

I am also grateful to Peter A. Frensch and an unknown referee for very helpful comments. I finished this book while visiting the University of Aberdeen, where I had inspiring discussions on working memory and problem solving with Robert Logie and Kenneth Gilhooly. I thank also Robert Logie and Mark Shackelton for correcting the language of the manuscript.

Chapter 1

Conceptual analysis

The cognitive revolution, the historical turn of psychology from observational concepts and language to concepts of mentalism and cognition, comprised a multitude of paradigmatic changes. In that period the introduction of broad new concepts was so rapid that they hardly had time to become established before something new was invented (Baars 1986). New methods such as simulation were adopted. Important theoretical problems such as attention, memory, imagery were discovered or rediscovered. Only a decade or two earlier, the same ideas had probably been considered as pseudoscience, but in the early 1960s the minds of researchers were open for novelties (e.g. Atkinson and Shiffrin 1968, Broadbent 1958, 1971, Cherry 1953, Miller 1956, Neisser 1967, Newell *et al.* 1958, 1963, Paivio 1971).

Like nuclear physics or inorganic chemistry, cognitive psychology constituted an autonomous research field, which independently defined its research topic, methods and theoretical concepts. The new approach concentrated on human information processing and replaced previously dominant topics such as conditioning (Neisser 1967, 1976, Newell and Simon 1972). Using experimental methods cognitive psychology concentrated on 'the activity of knowing: the acquisition, organization and use of knowledge' (Neisser 1976). Thinking, for example, has since been studied using theoretical concepts, methodological conventions and experimental paradigms that conceived the human mind as an information processing system (Anderson 1976, Bruner *et al.* 1956, Miller *et al.* 1960, Newell *et al.* 1958, Newell and Simon 1963, 1972).

When one looks at the time of the cognitive revolution in comparison with more recent developments in the field, a surprising conclusion is almost inevitable, namely that the main achievement of the time lay more in the number of new theoretical concepts than in dramatic experimental results. Indeed, when the results were dramatic, they were so mostly because important new concepts had been demonstrated. Nevertheless, the conceptual nature of the cognitive revolution is still poorly understood, in that no step has been taken towards advancing the research into the nature of conceptual work in cognitive psychology.

The current Kuhnian (1962) normal science with its fixed concepts and models appeared much later. The natural scientific viewpoint and dogmatic belief in conceptual systems was a product of the late 1970s and early 1980s. Newell's (1973b) worries about continuous diversification of the field and Broadbent's (1980) strong conservatism with respect to introducing new models are landmarks on the way towards a more established self-image. This has been coupled with a constantly growing reluctance to look critically at the assumed systems of concepts.

The movement from cognitive revolution to established cognitive psychology was unfortunately a jump out of the frying pan into the fire. Certainly the uncritical generation of theoretical concepts is unwise, as was pointed out during the late 1970s and early 1980s. Sadly, an equally serious error was made, in that practically all of the critical discussion concerning the nature of the basic concepts was buried under a superficially adopted 'philosophy of science'. In both cases the dialogue between the empirical and the conceptual was blocked.

As concepts determine the questions that can be asked, research into some important topics such as problem solving has been driven into a theoretical deadlock by overcautious attitudes toward concept development. New concepts can be found only by critically analysing the existing set of concepts, its weaknesses and strengths. Empirical research alone cannot replace conceptual analysis and concept formation. Experiments do not give definitions; on the contrary, definitions lead to experiments, and thus the critical analysis of basic theoretical concepts is decisive in the search for new research problems.

Of course, criticism of concepts, concept formation or conceptual analysis can never replace empirical work. There is no way of acquiring knowledge, testing theories and assessing the validity of concepts in psychology except by experimentation and observation. However, the effectiveness of empirical work depends on the questions that are asked, and these questions depend on concepts.

Consequently, active dialogue between the conceptual systems and empirical analysis is required in order to prevent experimentation from becoming a hollow routine, in which the same safe answers are constantly received in response to the same safe questions.

CAN HUMAN THINKING BE STUDIED USING GAMES?

In this book the main intention is to demonstrate in one task environment, chess, that real progress can be made in understanding human thinking by improving the conceptual system. By refining old concepts and adopting new ones, when necessary, the expressiveness of a scientific language can be improved and new ways of looking at the task environment can be found. To justify this approach, it is necessary first to show that it is reasonable to study thinking in a game environment such as chess.

The justification of single task environment studies has been recently criticized. Characteristically Earl Hunt (1991) has expressed severe doubts about the utility of chess and other games as task environments in problem-solving research. Though his position is untenable, he presents his case in a way that deserves very close attention. Hunt's paper is an important one, not because of his claim that games cannot be used in working with problem solving but because he was the first to ask metatheoretical questions when considering the state of current research on problem solving. This was a very useful insight, because it enabled him to raise a number of key questions. Even although Hunt's metatheoretical solutions are very traditional, it is probable that, by resolving the problems he poses in a more contemporary fashion, significant theoretical progress can be made.

Hunt (1991, pp. 391–2) writes:

Consider studies of how people play formal games, such as chess and bridge. Probably more attempts have been made to abstract general principles from the behavior in this area than in any area of complex problem solving. In reviewing the recent literature, French and Sternberg (this volume [1991]) repeat their argument that game playing is a useful thing to study because it serves as the *Drosophila* of cognitive science.

Does game playing serve this purpose? I doubt it. Geneticists have a theory that explains how one generalizes from inheritance in the fruitfly to inheritance in human beings. Cognitive psychology does not have a theory to explain how we move from game behaviors to behaviors in other situations. Indeed, there is a good deal to question [in] the generalization. . . . So how can we generalize from the board games to the board room?

This passage may appear as very poorly thought through. Hunt (1991) himself refers to the connection between working memory, chunking and expert problem solving, which is one of the core results in research on expertise, and which was shown first in chess (Chase and Simon 1973a, b, Djakov *et al.* 1926, de Groot 1965). This important breakthrough in chess studies has led to the finding of very similar connections between expertise, chunking and working memory capacity in numerous areas of expertise, and thus Hunt's (1991) claims about the futility of game research must be unfounded (see also Charness 1992, French and Sternberg 1991, Gilhooly and Green 1988, Holding 1985).

There are also other sources of evidence which testify to the success of game research. Neil Charness (1976), for example, managed to show that chess players do not store chess positions in working memory but in long-term memory. To my knowledge this was the first anomaly, in the Kuhnian (1962) sense, that put the Chase and Simon (1973a, b) theory of experts' working memory into question. More recently Ericsson and his collaborators have created a new paradigm and revised the whole theory of memory in experts (Chase and Ericsson 1981, 1982, Ericsson and Staszewski 1989, Ericsson and Kintsch 1994, Simon 1976). In any case, the critique of the old theory began by analysing human performance in a game.

Since the genetic similarity between *Drosophila* and man can hardly be much closer than the various areas of human expertise are to human cognition, I really cannot see that Newell and Simon's (1972) *Drosophila* metaphor would be misplaced. It is true, for example, that the genetic similarity of man and *Drosophila* operates at a molecular level, but the connections between games and real life operate on representational level and no essential metascientific difference can be shown. The literature shows that by studying just one game it is possible to glean evidence for cognitive structures that are similar over a large and varying set of task environments.

However, Hunt (1991) probably wants to make a deeper point, though he is not very explicit. It is unlikely that he wanted to put forward a thesis which can be refuted trivially, and thus I think that his criticism of game environments has a different target. In the pages following the above citation he discusses 'the dominance of the concrete', which means that in all the fields of complex problem solving the task-specific factors provide a more important basis for explanations than the general problem-solving methods. Consequently, the games, which are far from real-life and professional problem solving, cannot have much relevance for increasing our knowledge about the 'concrete' in managerial boards and other areas of expertise that are vital to life.

In Hunt's argument the term 'concrete' seems to refer to what is normally called information content, or at least some aspect of it. This point, i.e. the task-specific information content of problem solving, is as important as Hunt assumes it to be. However, his conclusion that game research could not have real significance in content-specific cognitive research is baseless. It is just an unhappy consequence of Hunt's belief in the misplaced but all too common research ideal which he calls 'scientific' [his quotation marks].

Hunt (1991) highlights in his paper important differences between science, engineering and humanistic research. Scientific knowledge is objective and general, engineering knowledge is objective but particular and humanistic knowledge is subjective and particular. The psychology of problem solving should pursue scientific knowledge but it has hardly achieved the level of engineering knowledge. The main reason for this unsatisfactory situation is that we have failed to find generalizations from simple environments to complex ones.

The overall scheme of Hunt's argument is admirably clear. Unfortunately, it is a closed system, to borrow his own term. This means that it works only as long as a certain set of tacit assumptions, indicative of the traditional empiricism, are accepted. In reality, the differences between the three practices are complicated. All the fields have numerous overlapping elements and the differences should be considered much more thoroughly, because the psychology of problem solving could greatly benefit from some elements that are characteristic of humanistic investigations. Hunt's (1991) traditional views of humanistic research simply prevent him from understanding how humanistic methods, such as conceptual analysis, could be applied in psychology.

Hunt rather carelessly simplifies both humanistic and natural scientific research by making a number of shallow points. First, he sees the natural scientific research process as observation and generalization of laws, which means that he does not pay any attention to the role of concepts in the research process. Second, Hunt assumes that humanistic research is subjective, because people may have differences of opinion about interpretation. This is equivalent to saying that natural scientific research is a superior research ideal as the researchers share a set of universal truths. Finally, he assumes that humanistic investigations pursue an insight, but not towards anything more objective. Since all these three points of common-sense metatheory are doubtful, though rather customary, they must be considered in some detail.

Hunt (1991, p. 384) writes: 'Scientific analysis takes place in two steps: the observation of empirical laws and the elucidation of general principles from which these laws can be derived.' This passage expresses the essence of Hunt's traditional empiricist metascience and the passage is the root of all the difficulties he has in trying to analyse the current state of complex problem-solving research. Important in Hunt's statement is not what is said but what is left out. By suggesting this two-level model for scientific analysis he forgets concepts and the concept formation process, which are the very core of all research and theory construction (Bunge 1967 might serve as a good introduction).

Presumably, Hunt (1991) is ignorant of the problems associated with observations being theory-laden (e.g. Hanson 1958). Though experiments provide us with objective observations, this does not mean that our theoretical conceptions do not affect the way the experiments are constructed and the way the results are interpreted. The behaviourists, for example, observed animals very differently from the Gestaltists, and their views about thinking were also contradictory (Köhler 1917/1957, Skinner 1957). Consequently, our observations are not independent of the pre-experimental theoretical concepts and thus disregard of conceptual analysis is unfounded and unwise.

Hunt's (1991) views are probably not at all rare among psychologists, though only a few of them are seriously interested in metascientific problems. Concepts are discussed in the current psychology so seldom that the conceptual underpinnings of observations are very probably seen as either non-existent, non-relevant, intuitive, or just matters of interpretation. The origin of these conceptually non-reflective views must lie in logical empiricism and related metascientific positions, in which dynamics of concepts had a relatively small function (Popper 1959, 1972, Suppe 1977). Unfortunately, this means that most of the important metascientific work since the mid-1950s has not materialized in the practical metascience of cognitive psychology (see, for example, Hanson 1958, Kuhn 1962, Lakatos 1970, Laudan 1977, Sellars 1956, 1963).

Paradoxically, Hunt (1991) could have understood the meaning of concepts if he had dug a little more deeply into the nature of humanistic investigations. Hunt argues that the differences of opinion between humanists are a sign of subjectivity. This means that he tacitly accepts the 'contraposition' according to which the apparently greater unanimity between natural scientists is a sign of a greater objectivity. True, natural scientists do agree about some things, but they have had, have at the moment, and will always have strong differences of opinion about many unsolved problems. The history of science provides a wealth of evidence for disagreements between natural scientists. The history of the theory of evolution might provide a very good example. The unity among natural scientists can be found in established research, but its existence in living research is an idealization.

A second problem with the idea of using the imagined unanimity among natural scientists, or, more precisely, its absence among humanists, is that it entails an elementary philosophical error. It implies that truth is a question which can be solved by unanimity of the 'experts' if not the unanimity of the 'populace'. As people have sometimes been all too unanimous, for example, over the shape of the earth or the correctness of behaviouristic thinking, we should finally bury the criteria of agreement and disunity. Truth and objectivity must be decided by arguing, not by voting. Consequently, Hunt's (1991) claim that the disunity of humanistic researchers is a sign of the subjectivity of the humanistic investigations proves to be illusory.

Hunt's (1991) idea of the humanistic research process as a 'pursuit towards insight' is even stranger than his subjectivity argument. Most serious humanistic investigation does not try to uncover feelings and casual truths but precise conceptual systems (e.g. Apel 1973, Gadamer 1975). In linguistics, for example, very definite categories are developed to describe various phenomena of language. Often these categories are valid in any language and not only in the particular one to which they are first applied (e.g. Chomsky 1965, Comrie 1983). Similar tendencies towards exact conceptual systems can be found in most fields of humanistic research. Indeed, in their pursuit of conceptual exactness the best humanistic researchers are much closer to mathematicians than to psychologists, who do not like to discuss their basic concepts.

Conceptual work is the aspect of humanistic research which psychology should adopt and apply. Humanistic research does not take its own concepts as eternally given, but as a subject for discussion. Even a brief look at the history of psychology, with constantly changing conceptual systems, should open our eyes to see that psychology may, after all, have something in common with humanistic research. Instead of walking around in the feathers of natural science psychologists should concentrate on the problems in their own conceptual systems. The only way out of the prevailing traditional empiricistic 'philosophy of science' inherited from the early 1950s is to carry out serious work on the theoretical concepts.

A connection between humanistic research and the psychology of thinking can hardly be a great surprise, because humanistic research directly works with the outcomes of human thinking and acting while natural scientists study the objects of nature. To argue a priori for the superiority of natural scientific methods when concerned with human thinking is not well founded. There are several ways of constructing combinations of the humanistic and scientific investigations within the psychology of thinking. Psychologists should be open-minded and avoid prejudging the issues.

ON CONCEPTUAL ANALYSIS

Scientific concepts are building blocks of theories (Bunge 1967). Concepts are the entities which distinguish intuitive knowledge from scientific knowledge and which organize scientific experience (e.g. Bunge 1967, Davidson 1984). They define what is essential and what is inessential in a particular context and provide the propositional knowledge with content. The concepts refer to something and enable people to separate their references out from all other available objects or actions, thus forming the very basis of human thinking. Concepts give the thoughts their contents, and by using spoken or written language people transmit these thoughts to each other.

Scientific concepts mostly are much more precise than everyday concepts, but this does not mean that they are free from intuitive elements. Their borders are not always effectively sharpened, and their references may be ambiguous. This is why constant special consideration should be devoted to the structure and content of concepts in any science. The basis of any analysis of this kind should always be the structure of the concepts themselves.

Concepts have several structural properties. They have attributes and they are combined with other concepts to form systems; that is, concepts have an internal attribute structure and an external structure of interconceptual relations. Both attributes and interconceptual relations can be expressed in propositional form. This means that attributes and interconceptual relations may be expressed as predicates of true propositions concerning the concept.

Even though attributes and interconceptual relations can be expressed in similar propositional forms, they are essentially different. Attributes are themselves concepts, which refer to necessary or accidental properties of a concept. Interconceptual relations define the relations between independent concepts. Thus, the proposition 'A dark background makes iconic representations last longer', for example, presents us with one attribute of iconic memory, and another proposition, 'The level of arousal is curvilinearly related to the capacity of attention', may serve as an example of an interconceptual relation. The effect of dark background is a property of iconic memory and special to it while arousal and capacity of attention may be interpreted as independent concepts because neither of them necessarily occurs in the same contexts as the other.

The contents of any theoretical concept embrace a set of propositions expressing either properties or interconceptual relations. This means that concepts themselves can be interpreted as nodes in large propositional networks. Indeed, this is very much how concepts have been seen in current cognitive psychology and cognitive science (Anderson and Bower 1973).

It is important to notice that interconceptual relations and internal attributes of the concepts form their contents. The contents of concepts are more important than their definition. A definition merely formulates the difference between one concept and other concepts which are semantically close. It does not provide much knowledge about the content of a concept; that is, its attributes and interconceptual relations. In fact, the very goal of the research process is to provide us with knowledge about the contents of concepts. In this sense, scientific knowledge is essentially conceptual and thus the historical development of a science means accumulation of its 'conceptual capital'.

Any psychological concept, such as attention, has its definition and its contents. Attention can be defined as selective perception or as the centre of perceptual experience (Broadbent 1958, Hochberg 1970). This definition, as definitions usually do, outlines the location of the concept being defined, in this case attention in relation to the concepts close to it. The definition implies, for example, that attention is not perception but a certain type of perceptual process. On the other hand, it implies also that attention as perceptual process is different from memory and thinking. However, not much more can be learned from any definition. Definitions do not provide us with knowledge about how to study attention or what are its most important attributes. All this must be achieved via empirical and conceptual work.

The contents of a concept cannot be inferred from its definition; they must be created by research. In practice this means that the concepts have a history: they evolve in the course of the research process. The current concept of learning, for example, has very little to do with the behaviouristic concept of learning. While the former was built on conditioning, the modern concept is normally grounded in memory (Bower 1975). Practically all psychological concepts are subject to a similar process of evolution.

Concepts are dynamic units. Their contents are in a state of constant change. The change is very dramatic during scientific revolutions. The birth of new paradigms requires the development of new scientific languages and conceptual systems (see, for example, Kuhn 1962 for the fate of concepts in scientific revolutions). The cognitive revolution is a very good example of a very swift change in the basic conceptual system. Nevertheless, the slow evolution of concepts during the periods of normal science is equally noteworthy. Our increased understanding of attention between the 1960s and today, for example, must be considered as seriously in the context of conceptual dynamics as the reintroduction of attention in the late 1950s.

Since concepts are dynamic, this should also be acknowledged in concrete research. Much more intensive efforts should be made to illuminate the contents and implications of concepts. During the 1980s cognitive psychology was not as succesful in improving its conceptual tools as it was during the 1950s and 1960s. The reason is simple. Currently very popular but outdated metascience simply does not give necessary weight to the concepts. This is why I think it is useful to remind cognitive psychologists about the difficulties hiding in the concepts, theoretical or observational, and to stress the special need for conceptual analysis.

The task of conceptual analysis is critically to consider the definitions, attributes, systems and history of actively used scientific concepts. Thus conceptual analysis must aim to improve the explications of concepts and, when necessary, to introduce new ones to fill gaps in the conceptual systems. Concept formation, sharpening, elucidation and interpretation are essential in conceptual analysis (Bunge 1967). Finally, we need to search for the possible tacit assumptions in concepts which may prevent us from fully understanding the phenomena.

The philosophical foundations and the ultimate justification of conceptual analysis can be found by studying Immanuel Kant's (1781) critical philosophy. He showed in an incontestable manner that our ability to acquire knowledge depends on our own reason. We are not random observers but we must actively use our reason to ask questions about nature. A citation from the *Critique of Pure Reason* might clarify Kant's position:

> When Galilei let balls of a particular weight, which he had determined himself, roll down an inclined plane, or Torricelli made the air carry a weight, which he had previously determined to be equal to that of a definite volume of water; or when, in later times, Stahl changed metal into lime, and lime again into metals, by withdrawing and restoring something, a new light flashed on all students of nature. They comprehended that reason has insight into that only, which she herself produces on her own plan, and that she must move forwards with the principles of her own judgements, according to a fixed law, and compel nature to answer her questions, but not let herself be led by the nature, as it were in leading strings, because otherwise accidental observations, made on no previously fixed plan, will never converge towards a necessary law, which is the only thing that reason seeks and requires.
>
> (Kant 1781/1966, pp. B XII–XIII)

The limits of our reason are also the limits of our empirical achievements, and the reason expresses itself in preconceived plans. However, the preconceived plans are nothing but theoretical concepts and theoretical systems. This means that we are not able to ask questions which surpass our conceptual capacity. This is why constant critical discourse on concepts is necessary in order to improve genuine scientific productivity. The ultimate significance of conceptual analysis is clear. No new problem area can be opened without conceptual analysis.

HOW TO USE CONCEPTUAL ANALYSIS

Conceptual analysis is a part of the thesis in this book. Not because this book is about conceptual analysis but because the problems which one meets in trying to improve our theoretical understanding of chess players' thinking and complex problem solving require the use of this method. To work towards new empirical findings in analysing chess players' thinking, it is inevitable that any researcher will work for new concepts, because the old concepts do not express what it is necessary to say.

This book tries to show how conceptual analysis can be used. It defines some new concepts, refines some old ones, and tests their validity in the analysis of the chess mind. This is what I believe conceptual analysis in an experimental psychology has to be. It is critical discussion about the basic concepts and developing alternatives followed by the analysis of empirical tradition. This is so because the ultimate goal of conceptual analysis is naturally an improved understanding of experimental data. To me this seems to be the most promising way to counter Hunt's (1991) critical views.

Hunt (1991) expressed severe doubts concerning the rationality of studying complex problem solving by using game environments. The problem was to him the problem of finding general laws and to this problem he could not find a solution. According to him it is doubtful whether game research could produce generalizable results and thus function as the fruitfly in the psychology of problem solving. When attention is moved from the laws to concepts, a new way of handling this problem can be presented.

When concepts are considered as they really are – that is, as dynamic building blocks of theoretical thinking – it is easy to see that the development of the conceptual organon of psychology is one of the main goals of research. Since conceptual systems can be developed and tested in a single environment and subsequently applied and modified in other environments, no logical reason exists why complex problem solving could not be studied by using formal games. Following Descartes' (1637/1975) ever true principle, it is wiser to begin with simple problems than with complex ones. Likewise the developing and testing of new concepts is better pursued in a task environment in which it can be done most effectively. This means that the right strategy is not to make careful obervations using the old conceptual system in new and socially important environments, but rather to develop the conceptual system itself, so that new ways of observing become possible. If the new concepts are valid and effective they open new questions.

The purpose of conceptual analysis is the improvement of the conceptual organon of psychology, because an improved conceptual system is a necessary precondition for an improved empirical understanding. In conceptual analysis postulation and sharpening of concepts is a method, but like any method it does not guarantee success. The rationality of concepts must be tested and the test is the quality of the empirical results and the validity of the theoretical analysis. The ultimate criterion is naturally the practice of scientific research and, indeed, life itself. Concepts which do not pass the test of practice are invalid, ineffective and should be abandoned.

If the concepts or systems of concepts that have been suggested are productive, new types of results can be found. If the system is not productive, it does not lead to essential improvements. Thus the results and conclusions of conceptual analysis are as testable as any element of scientific practice. There is no reason why the same critical reason could not be used in considering concepts as is used in considering procedures, observations and laws. Conceptual analysis is a rational part of scientific thinking and the avoidance of conceptual work in the name of 'scientificity' or some other reason is nothing but paving a way for dogmatism.

Chapter 2

Selective thinking and the models of chess mind

One goal of conceptual analysis is to break conceptual taboos and reveal holes in the conceptual systems. By a conceptual taboo I refer to concepts that could and should be discussed but remain unstudied because they do not belong to the established conceptual apparatus. Forgotten but sensible past concepts comprise one important class of conceptual taboos. Indeed, in the history of psychology one can find a number of important concepts that are hardly mentioned in the current literature. A notion like 'imagination' provides a good example of a conceptual taboo, in that it has been under intensive discussion for centuries, but seems to have been lost from current practice.

Often the reason why a taboo arises seems to be that the concepts are outside the scope of current methodology. This is a very good reason indeed, since there is no point in asking unanswerable questions. However, sometimes the reason for a taboo is much less defensible. Some concepts may be accidentally forgotten. In this latter case it is very important to start working with the old ideas using modern methodical, theoretical and conceptual apparatus.

Conceptual analysis is necessary when the introduction of a new concept or reintroduction of an old concept is required. Often, no recent theoretical standpoint clarifying a new concept can be found and the discussion about the concept must begin by analysing pretheoretical or lay psychological intuitions, working with historical conception and connecting the concept with available knowledge. When for decades no serious work has been done to sharpen a concept, theoretical characterizations are needed. Undoubtedly the basic theoretical characterization is one task for conceptual analysis in psychology.

The first taboo I shall try to break concerns selective thinking.

Though most psychologists in the field very probably admit that thinking is selective, which can be seen in the wide use of concepts such as heuristics, rationality, illusions, etc., a search of the Psychlit database revealed that practically nothing is being done at the moment to study selectivity directly. The minimal recent research interest in selective thinking makes it necessary to start from the very beginning. It must first be demonstrated that selective thinking is an intuitively plausible and important problem. Next we must discover how selective thinking was dealt with before cognitive psychology came along. Third, arguments must be presented to support the claim that the concept of selectivity might be of real use in modern cognitive psychology. If these three conditions can be fulfilled, the problem of selectivity is conceptually justified.

Conceptual justification is, however, only a beginning. The most important stage in introducing a new concept is to build the connections between the concept and concrete empirical knowledge. Without a link with empirical research, a concept is not worth much, because it is very probably not researchable by current methods. This means also that no attributes can be attached to the concepts and thus the concept must be left empty.

In this book, I shall try to build the connection between empirical research and the concept of selective thinking in the context of chess players' thinking. Therefore, to build the foundations for this endeavour, a task analysis of chess must be carried out and after that the main theories of chess players' thinking must be reviewed. In this way it is possible to find out whether a connection can be forged between the concept of selective thinking and current empirical material. An overview of the previous theories is also needed to uncover the difficulties encountered by earlier theorists, and what would be the most reasonable way to approach the problem of selective thinking.

IS THE PROBLEM OF SELECTIVE THINKING A SENSIBLE PROBLEM?

Unlike perception, thought is not stimulus-bound and may refer to the past or future, to invisible objects, to abstract concepts and complex physical or social systems. Unlike perception too, the contents of thought need not be directly related to the present environment. Thus it can be limited only by limits in the power of the human mind to obtain and to criticize ideas. Thinking is free from the immediate environment, but this freedom makes selectivity twice as important. Thought can represent the world only in one way at a time and thus it must select from among a huge number of alternatives, which is what makes human thinking selective.

Selectivity of thinking is a general problem. Therefore, all traditional schools of psychology have tacitly and sometimes quite explicitly addressed it. However, it is evident that they have been able to find just fragments of all the mechanisms that are characteristic of human selective thinking. To connectionists and behaviourists such as Thorndike (1911), Hull (1943), Maltzman (1955) and Berlyne (1965), selective thinking was basically the application of learned response tendencies in familiar and unfamiliar situations. This means that these researchers were able to show the relevance of recognition for selective thinking. Yet they had very little, if anything, to say about the original discrimination and formation of new response tendencies.

To the Gestaltists, selectivity was one of the most basic concepts and hence selective thinking was a natural problem for them. They showed with numerous elegant and evergreen experiments how the perceptual organization of a visible problem situation could change with a sudden insight or how serious errors could follow from subjects' inability to restructure the perceptual field (Duncker 1945, Koffka 1935, Köhler 1917/1957, Wertheimer 1945). However, the strong perceptual orientation of the Gestaltists made them less interested in thinking when no direct visual input was involved (for an exception see Wertheimer 1945). Consequently, for them the contents of thought were a marginal problem.

Finally, schema theorists worked on developing a theory in which perceptual stimulus processing and thought were controlled by learned internal schemata (Bartlett 1932/1977, 1958, Piaget 1952, Selz 1913, 1924). They developed important concepts such as 'expectation' and 'constraints'. However, the concrete contents of thought were not of major importance to schema theorists. They really had no clear idea how different information contents could co-operate in constructing internal representations. Thus, schema theorists paid attention to the problem of selectivity but the notion of schemata made their analysis often abstract and not content specific.

Cognitive psychology has inherited most of the major theoretical problems of its predecessors and the problem of selective thinking among them. Numerous established experiments and 'research

programmes' tacitly document the relevance of selective information processing for cognitive theories of thought. Illusions and other
decision errors, reasoning fallacies and failures in problem-solving
tasks may serve as examples (Barron 1988, Evans 1982, 1989,
Johnson-Laird 1983, Johnson-Laird and Byrne 1991, Newell and
Simon 1972, Payne 1982, Tversky and Kahneman 1974, VanLehn
1990). Thus selective thinking looks very much like a cognitive
problem. None the less, the problem of selective thinking has very
seldom been mentioned in the cognitive literature. The reason can
only be that the notion of selectivity has been considered to be
unclear, or too difficult to address. This is unfortunate, because
empirical research in cognitive psychology would give a very
strong basis for any analysis of selective thinking (Evans 1989).

The psychology of thinking is not theoretically consistent today.
No overall theory of thinking exists, but the major thought processes
such as problem solving, reasoning, decision making and concept
formation are independent and have few, if any, theoretical connections (see, for example, Mayer 1983). This task-based theoretical
conceptualization originates from the behaviourist era. Then it was
logical to classify phenomena on the grounds of the stimulus
situations but today it appears as increasingly more artificial. What
would be needed in a cognitive theory of thinking would be concepts
that make it possible to generalize beyond the boundaries of the task-
environments. In the long run, it is likely that selectivity could be a
concept of real use in constructing more general theories of thinking.

The work on selectivity in thinking can be conceptually justified.
However, conceptual justification is merely one way of posing the
problem. It can add very little to the content of a concept, and
therefore conceptual justification must be followed by empirical
analysis. In this book the empirical analysis is made in one task,
problem solving, and one task environment, chess. However, when
we better understand selective thinking in chess, we will certainly be
better able to develop theories that describe selective thinking in
other task environments as well.

WHAT MAKES CHESS A SUITABLE TASK
ENVIRONMENT TO STUDY SELECTIVE THINKING?

Several reasons can be presented as to why chess is particularly
suitable for the psychological study of selective thinking (Charness
1992, Newell and Simon 1972). First, chess is an easily controllable

but reasonably demanding task environment. The finite and discursive nature of chess aids researchers in generating non-trivial, well-defined and meaningful problems that have unique solutions. Finding a move in chess is not a task in which all information is available. Chess players must often make their decisions like managers under circumstances of uncertainty, because the complexity of chess positions mostly does not allow chess players to calculate all variations to a conclusion. They do not know what will be over the horizon of the calculable move sequences and they must make their move choices on the grounds of highly conceptual but uncertain chess-strategic information (see, for example, Berliner 1974, Saariluoma and Hohlfeld 1994).

The second reason for the use of chess in studying selective thinking is skill differences. They are important, as they help to provide controllable variation. The strongest chess players are usually professionals or semi-professionals. They have worked thousands of hours to acquire their skill, and consequently they have evolved task-specific knowledge bases that are considerably more sophisticated than are those of moderately skilled players or novices. The skill differences thus allow researchers to analyse conceptual systems at different levels, which makes it easier to obtain information about the underlying processing system (Chase and Simon 1973a,b, Holding 1985, Newell and Simon 1972). Comparisons between masters and novices are very useful, and in particular the extreme skill conditions provided by grandmasters furnish researchers with a special perspective on selectivity in thinking (see Hintikka 1969 for the benefits of extreme conditions). In brief, experts 'sample' the same stimulus very differently from novices, and this is very helpful in the search for the mechanisms of selectivity.

The objectivity of chess ensures a very precise measure for skill differences. Chance and luck, it is widely acknowledged, play practically no role in chess, and thus any measurement based on performance of the players is objective (see, for example, Charness 1992, Wagenaar 1988). The measurement system in general use was designed by Arpad Elo (1965, 1978) and is called the ELO rating system. This system is used worldwide in slightly different forms. The great benefit of this system for psychological research is its international comparability and objectivity. Experiments made in any country are directly and reliably comparable with respect to skill level all over the world.

The idea of the ELO rating system is very simple. It assumes that better players win with a greater probability than weaker ones and that equal players when meeting each other both score approximately 50 per cent of the points. The larger the difference between two players, the more likely it is that the better player will win. Each player is given a numeric value that expresses his or her place among all other players. The difference in these ELO ratings between any two players expresses the probability that one of them will win (Elo 1978). Players' rating will rise when they win. It rises more the larger the difference between the player and the opponent. If the player loses, the rating is deducted correspondingly. In the case of a draw, the weaker player will gain points and the stronger will lose them. Accordingly, the skill level of each player can be determined after a few games. (The details of the system can be found in Elo 1965 and 1978, and its main lines have been explained in Holding 1985. Batchelder and Bershad 1979 and Batchelder and Simpson 1988 also provide important information about the ELO rating system.)

The third attractive feature of chess is that chess players have developed highly automatized habits for verbalizing their thoughts. They may spend hours discussing and analysing board positions with their competitors or team mates, which greatly improves their capacity to express their ideas verbally. This is, of course, a very important advantage because it is often hard to get subjects to verbalize their thoughts (Ericsson and Simon 1980, 1984, Newell 1977). The fourth argument for working with chess players is the chess culture itself, which is very psychologically oriented. Chess players have clearly understood the practical importance of psychology in chess (Krogius 1976, Pfleger and Treppner 1988). There are many legends in chess circles about world champions and their psychological insights, and a good number of these can be found in two books, respectively by Hartston and Wason (1983) and by Munzert (1989). Emmanuel Lasker, of course, is the most famous of all world champions in this respect (Reti 1933). For example, he was known to pursue good moves rather than ideal moves. As a mathematician he understood that the complexity of chess makes it impossible to search for ideal moves, and so the resources invested in finding the ideal move would prevent a player from searching even for good moves in some later stage of the game (Reti 1933). The idea clearly resembles Simon's (1956, 1983) famous principle of bounded rationality.

On the other hand, chess folklore is very often mythical, uncritical and superstitious, and these uncontrolled fantasies make it necessary to take a very critical attitude when chess players' psychological ideas are considered from a scientific point of view. Some grand-masters, for example, defended themselves against Mikhail Tal's 'hypnotic gaze' by wearing sunglasses – to little effect, however, because Tal became a world champion.

Finally, the highly conceptual character of chess provides special perspectives for studying conceptual information selection in chess. Only people who have devoted substantial effort into learning the nuances of chess are able to find them in stimulus positions, though everybody can perceive them. This means that individual differences are conceptual, and thus they provide a very good platform to study non-perceptual selective thinking.

CHESS – THE TASK ENVIRONMENT

Chess has the formal structure of a tree. A tree is a collection of arcs and nodes. The arcs connect the nodes to each other. In a tree, each node has one ancestor, though it may have any number of children. In a game tree (Figure 2.1) one node is called a root and all the other nodes are its children or the children of its children. Thus, a game tree is a directed graph (e.g. Stanat and McAllister 1977). Likewise, a chess position can be seen as a node and a move as an operator represented by an arc.

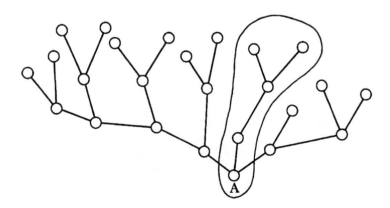

Figure 2.1 Game tree and one branch. 'A' refers to the current position

From a game theoretical point of view, chess is a finite game. Its rules guarantee that no game can be continued indefinitely. The game tree of chess is deep, but not even close to infinite, since the longest imaginable game with modern rules has been assessed to be some 6,500 moves (Böök 1967). Normal tournament games are very seldom over 100 moves long, and the typical number of moves is around 40 (de Groot 1966, Holding 1979, 1985). Nevertheless, the total size of the game tree in chess is enormous, and the estimated size of the tree is in the range of 10 to the power of 120 nodes (Charness 1977, Newell and Simon 1972). This is sufficient to prevent modern computers from finding solutions (Newell and Simon 1972).

Chess is a two-player game with perfect information and with no chance moves. This means that a position in chess contains all the information that is needed to make a correct choice of move. In poker, for example, some of the information is hidden. Chess is also a pure conflict game in which no co-operation is involved, which means that opponents compete to beat one another.

In principle, chess belongs to the type of games that in game theory are often considered trivial (Simon 1974b, c). However, in practice the difference between the actual game and the mathematical theory is quite wide. Research into logical thinking has shown very clearly that the behaviour of normal people does not follow the rules of formal logic (e.g. Evans 1982, 1989, Johnson-Laird and Byrne 1991, Wason and Johnson-Laird 1972), and, similarly, game theoretical notions have only a restricted relevance for chess players' thinking (Simon 1974b, c).

In game theory, a winning strategy comprises a procedure that aids a player to select the best move in each node of a game tree. In principle, chess allows for such a strategy. Assuming that both parties always chose their best moves, it should be possible to say whether the initial position is a forced win for White, or for Black, or a draw. However, no such strategy has been found so far and the ideal solution for chess is unknown. The size of the game tree has prevented the finding of any winning strategy.

Some game theoretical aspects of losing moves have been considered by Simon (1974b, c). He suggests that a game can be represented by a lattice-like structure. In this structure White's correct move is always to the upper left and Black's correct move to the right. If both players make correct moves the game ends in a draw. If White errs that player has selected a move that directs his or her pieces towards the upper right, moving the course of the game towards the edge, i.e. towards defeat. If a player makes more errors, before long he or she is in a situation that cannot be saved even with the best play. Simon's (1974b, c) analysis shows very clearly why errors are crucial in practical chess play and why the human factor is so vital.

Simon's analysis requires one comment. Not all losing moves have equal consequences. A move that loses a pawn is mostly a less serious error than one that loses the queen. The worse the move the more difficult it is to get back into the game. In practice, this means that one move can spoil everything. On the other hand, a bad move, even though not objectively the best, can put the opponent into a difficult position. If there is no easy path to a draw or a victory, a difficult position may lead the opponent to make errors (Reti 1933).

THEORIES OF CHESS SKILL

Psychologists have deliberated chess skill theoretically several times during this century. A number of theoretical constructs have been presented. They have mainly followed the conceptualizations that have been in vogue at the time. Thus Cleveland (1907) followed the ideas of Stout (1896), de Groot (1965) followed the ideas of Selz (1913, 1924), and Newell and Simon (1972) followed as well as contributed to the general development of cognitive concepts.

Chess has interested psychologists mainly as an example of an intellectual skill. The researchers have studied it to find information about intelligence, memory and thinking (Baumgarten 1930, Doll and Mayr 1987). Age effects and life spans of chess players have been regularly studied (Baumgarten 1930, Charness 1981a, b, c, 1985, 1991, Chi 1978, Elo 1965, 1978, Lehman 1953, Weinert *et al.* 1987). The motivational structures and professional backgrounds of chess players have also been the subject of interest among psychologists (S. Carey, personal communication 1993, Fine 1956, Gobet 1992, de Groot 1965, Horgan 1992, Horgan and Morgan 1989, Jones 1987).

The research into individual differences has so far shown that chess players are not cognitively exceptional people. They just happen to have a passion for the game. Their skill is a consequence of a decade or so of training, and chess players do not show any general intellectual superiority, being of normal academic ability (Elo 1978, de Groot 1965, Hayes 1981, 1985). The normality of chess players' background variables naturally supports claims that chess is a good task environment for studying how the thinking of people changes during the course of acquiring cognitive skills.

CLEVELAND'S SKILL ACQUISITION MODEL

The first model of the chess mind was suggested by Cleveland (1907). His theory contains many important characteristics of the modern theories of chess skill. Although the empirical evidence behind the theory is on the whole casual and uncritical by current standards, many of Cleveland's theoretical suggestions and ideas are very plausible.

The main part of Cleveland's theory concentrates on skill acquisition. He suggests a five-stage model of skill development analogous to Bryan and Harter's (1899) still recognized theory of telegraphic skill development (see, for example, Shiffrin 1988). The first stage is to learn the names and movements of the pieces. This subskill is later automatized. The second stage may be characterized as the stage of individual offensive and defensive moves during which a beginner plays with no definite aim other than to capture pieces. At this stage blunders and overlooked moves are common. Play is casual since players are without broader goals. In the third stage they learn the values of the pieces. They also learn the most primitive strategic plans. In the fourth stage the importance of development appears: that is, the moving of pieces very swiftly from their initial positions into battle. Finally, the whole process culminates in the acquisition of 'positional sense'.

Though Cleveland's (1907) theory contains notable ideas about the accumulation of subskills, the argument is unclear. Strategic information, for example, is often based on qualitatively different types of cues as compared with tactical information. The strategic notion of development, for example, does not automatically follow from the increased ability to detect threats. Development of pieces in chess requires paying attention to the number of pieces in their original squares and the number of moves needed to reach full development. This piece of knowledge has very little to do with threats. Strategic cues are qualitatively different from movement patterns, and therefore it is hardly justified to argue that strategic skills would emerge from improved tactical skill.

Cleveland paid much attention to selectivity and understood the role of recognition in chess players' thinking. He wrote: 'Skill in the middle game is shown by the readiness with which he [a player] recognizes the essential features of a new situation, and, in his inner experimentation, hits upon a move that fits the case' (Cleveland, 1907, p. 293). In this way he suggested the idea that later and in a more sophisticated form became the core of recognition–action models (Chase and Simon 1973b). Following Stout (1896), Cleveland briefly mentions apperception to describe the formation of the contents of thought:

> Increase in skill means increase in the knowledge of chess situations and how to meet them; or, in more psychological terms, increasing 'meaning' in certain arrangements of the pieces, and increased facility of association between these meaningful arrangements and certain other arrangements (moves to be made) imaginatively constructed; or still in other terms, more adequate apperception of situations and richer and better organized associations connected therewith.
>
> (1907, p. 293)

This short paragraph shows Cleveland's clear understanding of the connection between selectivity and skill. The experts are experts because they are able to apperceive the meaning in middle game arrangements better than novices. However, his conception of apperception is classical and not particularly original. He is, for example, unable to specify the mechanisms that could be responsible for apperceiving meaningful arrangements.

Cleveland's (1907) theory contains a number of very clever ideas. He argues for selectivity, meaningfulness of patterns, recognition and the mechanisms of skill development, which all are current and relevant problems even today. The problem with his theory is its inability to give detailed information about the mechanisms behind the meaningfulness and information selection. The overall reference to recognition is not a satisfactory answer.

DE GROOT'S SYSTEM

De Groot's (1965) theoretical thinking is based on Otto Selz's (1913, 1924) ideas on human problem solving, but de Groot gives them a particularly chess specific interpretation. Thanks to his Selzian orientation, de Groot is inevitably confronted with the problem of selectivity in thinking. He is interested in the differences in the number of generated moves, thus providing empirical information about the very strong selectivity of chess players' thinking. He also concerns himself with the transition, assimilation of knowledge, expectations and anticipation, which are all themes linked with selective thinking.

In de Groot's (1965) theory the alternation between what he calls integrative and elaborative phases is central. Each transformation between the two phases leads to a deeper conception of the problem and the total goal concept; that is, the solver's way of conceiving the problem is elaborated. Transformation refers thus in current terminology to a change in the contents of the representation. Examples of common transformations are insight, progressive deepening, trying out, stipulating the order of investigations, and typical ways of reasoning.

De Groot (1965) also gives the transformations a methodological status. This is one of the critical points in his theory. All the transformations are undoubtedly typical of problem-solving processes, but they are hardly methods in the current sense. A method is a consciously selected way of behaving. In psychology, for example, the experimental method is a consciously adopted way of approaching the human mind. However, insight or trying out are far from being consciously controlled. There is no way in which we can decide to use insight. Therefore, it is not right to think of de Groot's problem-solving methods as methods in precisely the same sense as the word is normally used. They are types of information processes or forms of behaviour rather than means–ends like strategies (Newell and Simon, 1972).

In addition to general problem-solving methods, de Groot (1965) discussed briefly what he called 'playing methods'. They include the chess-specific knowledge of the chess masters from stereotypical combinations to strategic ideas and opening theory. However, he never really specifies these factors and their role in thinking. De Groot did not try to find a cognitive and representation-based explanation for the empirical phenomena he found, and thus the content-specific aspects of chess players' thinking were not very important to him.

De Groot's (1965) investigations into memory are very interesting, though they follow earlier work by Djakov *et al.* (1926). De Groot was able to demonstrate experts' superiority in recalling real game positions. These memory studies were theoretically very important, because they gave the research into chess skill and expertise a new direction and they brought expertise and the concept of capacity into the centre of the research. Experts differed from novices because they could remember better chess positions and they could remember chess positions better, having practised chess.

De Groot's (1965) empirical description of chess players' behaviour is very precise. He was able to show convincingly the connection between skill and information-processing capacity. On the other hand he could not really analyse the contents of chess players' thinking in the modern sense. The conceptual apparatus of precognitive psychology could not provide him with suitable conceptual tools for this kind of analysis.

HEURISTIC SEARCH MODELS

With chess-playing computer programs, the problem of selective thinking becomes in a new way the key problem in the field. It was not possible to use a British Museum Algorithm-like exhaustive search algorithm in chess, but it was necessary to find effective means to separate the best move sequences from all possible sequences (Newell and Simon 1972). It was also noticed that human search is highly selective. People did not pay any attention to the irrelevant alternatives and consequently could easily beat the chess-playing programs of the early 1960s. Consequently, the problem of selective search in man and machines became a very popular problem.

The first solution to the selection problem was heuristic search (Shannon 1950, Turing 1950). The operating heuristic search model of chess players' thinking was introduced in the late 1950s by Newell *et al.* (1958, 1963). Heuristic search models were also the first computational models of human thinking (Newell *et al.* 1958). They were meant to be very rough analogies, but they opened a new method in presenting theoretical concepts and models in psychology, namely computer simulation (Newell and Simon 1972, 1976).

Chess players' selective thinking could now be conceived of as a heuristic search (Newell and Simon 1963, 1972). In these models chess players' problem solving comprises search in the basic problem space. The move selection is based on heuristic evaluation rules. In each node the program generates all the legally possible moves and thereafter it evaluates all the moves using some heuristic rules. The evaluation value is very often just a sum or a weighted sum of the evaluation dimensions. If the search is a best-first search,

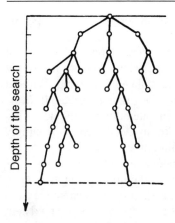

Figure 2.2 Heuristic search. The best alternative is selected from a number of evaluated alternatives, and search is continued similarly from that node on
Source: Botvinnik (1984)

the highest evaluated move is made on the imaginary board and the search continues in the same way until some upper limit, such as the horizon, or the solution, is found (Figure 2.2).

Several variations of heuristic search models have been suggested. Mostly they are not meant to be precise models of human thinking processes, but rather demonstrations of the possibilities offered by heuristic problem solving. The argument was not that human thinking would be very similar to early heuristic search programs, but rather that human heuristics were much more effective than anything realized with a computer (Newell and Simon 1972, 1976).

A good example of psychologically quite interesting heuristic search programs was MATER. It is a program that searches for a checkmate (Newell and Simon 1972). MATER uses one heuristic rule. It looks through all the check moves or, in advanced form, all check moves at a depth of two moves. Thus if a mate can be achieved through a series of check moves MATER can find it. MATER is intriguing, because it contains in a very early form the idea of subspace abstraction. It concentrates solely on one part of the large network of moves in a checkmate position, and thus the simulations in suitable positions look very human-like. In this way MATER demonstrates that human-like selectivity is not impossible for computers, if only we knew the underlying content-specific semantics.

The weaknesses of the early heuristic search models as models of human thinking soon became obvious. They could not explain planning, which is so important in chess players' thinking. Without planning, chess players cannot restrict their search spaces. In heuristic search models subjects should generate all the available moves in a node position to be able to make an evaluation. This simply does not happen in chess players' thinking.

According to heuristic search models subjects should also use intermediate node evaluation. That is, in the protocols at each level of depth after a generated move, one should find evaluative sentences. But this in practice is either very rare or non-existent (Saariluoma 1990b, Saariluoma and Hohlfeld 1994). People may simulate that kind of behaviour but normally evaluative sentences appear at the very end of the episodes. The function of such statements is to evaluate the generated continuation as a whole rather than an individual move (Newell and Simon 1972).

A third piece of evidence against heuristic search models can be found from eye-movement studies. Human eye movements are highly selective and they concentrate on some key areas of the board position (Simon and Barenfeld 1969, Tikhomirov 1988, Tikhomirov and Poznyanskaya 1966). Heuristic search models would predict that the eye movements would be distributed quite evenly over the board, because heuristic searchers generate all the moves at a depth of one before evaluating. Consequently, heuristic search models, despite their good performance in playing chess, are inadequate models of the human mind. The use of operators in heuristic search models is too static compared to human chess players.

The evidence against heuristic search models is clear-cut. They cannot explain human selectivity, though it is a very good basis for computer chess-playing programs. The working computer program is not, unfortunately, as such a working model of human mental processes, because computer programs do not give unambiguous information (Anderson 1976). Though the behaviour of a program may be very human-like this does not mean that the same behaviour could not be the result of some very different type of process in the human mind.

The crucial omission from heuristic search models was that they had little or nothing to say about the semantic organization of chess players' thinking. They were thus just mechanical models, which were very helpful in developing such basic concepts as problem space and search, but could achieve nothing more (cf. Simon 1979).

RECOGNITION–ACTION MODELS

In the early 1970s a new type of model termed 'production systems' was introduced in the psychology of chess. Production systems are formalisms that have been developed on the basis of Post's work. They were suggested by Newell and Simon (1972) to be the basic model for studying human planning (Anderson 1976, Newell 1973b, 1990). Their suggestion was widely accepted and, for some time, production systems have provided a very interesting tool for modelling mind (Allport 1980a, b, Anderson 1976, 1983).

Production systems normally consist of the long-term memory with a large number of production rules and working memory supplied with data. The production rules have an 'if . . . then' form, with two parts called respectively the pattern and the action parts. The pattern part expresses some task-specific pattern and the action part expresses some task-specific action (Figure 2.3).

The key idea of production systems is very simple. If there is an active environmental pattern in working memory, it activates the corresponding production in long-term memory. The action part of an activated production is then carried out. The action changes the situation, so that a new pattern enters working memory and a further action can be accomplished. In this way production systems are procedural models of human cognition (Allport 1980a,b, Anderson 1976, 1983).

A production systems based recognition–action model (the term was introduced by Holding 1985) of chess players' search was suggested by Newell and Simon (1972) and Chase and Simon

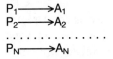

Figure 2.3 Production system. A set of productions in long-term memory with pattern (P) and action (A) parts and corresponding actions. Long-term memory is communicating with the patterns in working memory by activating relevant productions and manipulating the information content of working memory by the action of action parts

(1973b). Their idea was uncomplicated: knowledge in a chess player's memory is represented by productions. When a chess player sees a familiar pattern of pieces referring, for example, to a tactical trick such as a knight fork, the initial pattern activates the corresponding series of moves. Chase and Simon (1973a,b) supported their production systems theory with an argument based on the working memory capacity of chess players. They pointed out that in recall experiments experts could remember chess positions better than novices, because they had a huge store of chess-specific patterns in their long-term memory. If experts had more chess-specific patterns in their memories, they had also more productions. This directly implies that experts also have a higher probability of finding strong moves.

Production systems have met some as yet unsolvable problems, two of which normally stand out. The first is the problem of matching. How and when is an environmental pattern equal to a pattern in long-term memory? Environments usually vary to the degree that it is hard to store all the required patterns in the computer's memory. The other problem is conflict resolution. This means simply that a situation may activate several productions at the same time, and the system must be able to decide which one is correct or most effective.

Since no general solutions to the problems with production systems have been found, the recognition–action model has failed as a model of chess players' thinking. The model is simply too mechanistic. The search is totally plan guided and not particularly flexible. This kind of model may describe how routine plans are applied, but it says very little, if anything at all, about creative problem solving.

HOLDING'S SEEK THEORY

According to Holding (1985), the recognition–action model is far too mechanistic (see also Dreyfus 1972, 1992, Dreyfus and Dreyfus 1986). Holding and Reynolds (1982) showed that chess players' recall of chess positions did not necessarily correlate with their problem-solving capacity. Skilled chess players are better than non-skilled players in recalling game positions but not in recalling random positions, yet they may be clearly better in solving problems in pseudorandom positions.

Holding's (1985) conclusions were straightforward: pattern-based thinking should be abandoned. He also argued that the number of assumed patterns in chess experts' memory could not be as large as was thought. Furthermore, genuine search could not be neglected in building models for chess players' problem solving. In Holding's (1985) theory search and evaluation constitute the essence of chess players' skill, and the true source of skill differences is in the experts' ability to search longer variations and make more precise evaluations. The recognition of familiar patterns and positions is of secondary value.

SEEK assumes that skilled chess players use their knowledge to generate alternatives. This requires three components: search, evaluation and knowledge. The differences among these components are decisive in discriminating between experts and novices. In this way SEEK emphasizes a kind of total conception of chess thinking.

The weakness of Holding's (1985) SEEK is its intuitive nature. One could also say that it is very much a precognitive model, because it does not make representational assumptions. Holding (1985) does not provide any precise mental or cognitive principles by which the search is controlled, nor does he present any information about how evaluations are carried out. Could it be that the recognition of familiar features had something to do with the mechanisms of evaluation, despite the fact that the theory does not reserve a key role for recognition? The model is thus open to several alternative interpretations.

Holding's (1985) theory can be interpreted as a heuristic search model, in which node evaluation is essential. In his later writings Holding (1989, 1992a, b) has emphasized the meaning of planning in search, and so the theory seems to be moving towards the idea of a plan-guided search, but the absence of representational assumptions decreases the explanatory power of the theory. As a consequence of its non-cognitivism SEEK has very little to say about the internal structure of search and evaluation and it is unable to postulate any mechanisms for selective thinking.

THE COGNITIVE PROBLEM OF SELECTIVE THINKING

In many respects the complexity of the game tree in chess and the conceptual character of chess players' thinking make chess an ideal task enviroment in which to study selective thinking. Chess psychologists have also understood this. From Cleveland (1907) to Holding (1985), chess psychologists have argued for the significance of selective thinking in chess. De Groot (1965) made very precise empirical observations in order to study selectivity, and Newell and Simon (1972) introduced computational methods for modelling selective thinking. This suggested that heuristic search or pattern recognition might explain how selective thinking is possible. Still, only the surface of the problems has been tackled properly. Holding's (1985) partial return to a precognitive approach is a sign of conceptual and theoretical cul-de-sac.

How is it possible that after so long and such determined work on selectivity in the chess mind, we have not been able to resolve this problem in a more satisfactory way? Why are we unable to explain how the small move networks are constructed? What controls the human mind so that, by generating just a fraction of moves as compared to computers, the mind still holds its own and the day when computers beat world champions has been so long coming? Why has the momentum of the 1960s and the early 1970s in the analysis of chess players' thinking ceased, though there are probably more researchers working on the problem than ever before? The answer must be in the theoretical concepts themselves. They are not sufficiently productive.

If the problem is conceptual, as I think it to be, the right way to make progress is to apply conceptual analysis. The problem is where to begin. What concepts should be considered to find further information about selectivity? Where should we apply conceptual analysis to improve the efficiency of the conceptual system? No standard answer to these questions can be given.

The concept of selectivity is not only related to thinking; it can be found in attention and memory research as well. Attention research is research into selective perceiving, and sometimes one can find references to selective access in memory. The use of the term selectivity would thus suggest that one must heed the very basic notions of attention and memory on which so much of cognitive psychology is built. One must study what it is that research into chess players' attention and memory may explain about selective thinking in chess. What is attentional or memory based in this process and what is not, is a question of prime importance. After knowing what in selective thinking can be explained using the attributes of attention and memory, the main focus may be directed to thinking itself.

If the main properties of selective thinking cannot be reduced to attention or memory, one must ask what is wrong with the current concepts of the psychology of thinking that they cannot provide a sufficient basis for analysing selective thinking. If recognition alone, or recognition together with other memory processes, provides an insufficient basis for managing selective thinking (as was tried by Chase and Simon 1973, a, b for example), new and more expressive concepts must be acquired. Presumably these concepts must be developed within the psychology of thinking.

Before we move on to search for new concepts for the psychology of thinking it is best to find the conceptual reasons why the attempts to reduce much of thinking to memory processes have failed. This means that one must carefully analyse the attributes of attention and memory. The empirical findings and theoretical insights in the research into chess players' attention and memory must be judged *sub specie* selective thinking. It is necessary to understand what the main properties of chess attention and memory are, and what these properties may tell us about selective thinking in chess.

Only if conceptual analysis finally shows that some aspects of selective thinking are inexplicable in terms of the current attentional and memory research must one start searching the properties of thinking, which may resolve the problems, or at least show a pathway for finding the solution.

This 'onion peeling' strategy begins with the idea that the basic cognitive functions, such as attention and memory, are essential concepts in the system of interconceptual relations of selective thinking. Thus their analysis should make explicit essential problems in the system of implicit conceptual problems in the previous research into the chess mind and selective thinking in chess. Moreover, if the reduction of selective thinking to attention and memory fails, the points at which the failure happens presumably provide essential information about the thinking itself.

Chapter 3

Attention in chess players' thinking

Chess players have always had an intuitive understanding of the important role of attentional processes in thinking (Abrahams 1951, Krogius 1976). All too often games are lost by overlooking something obvious. This everyday experience has taught chess players the role of attention in their thinking. Chess players' intuitions are by no means scientific but the importance of attention is supported by a number of objective results from the psychology of problem solving. Consequently, attention in chess is an issue that deserves closer scrutiny.

Scientifically, attention refers to selective perception (Allport 1989, Broadbent 1958, Navon 1989a, b, Shiffrin 1988, van der Heijden 1990). The intuition behind the notion of attention is very clear. People are thought to perceive some stimuli rather than others or some particular aspects of a stimulus. Thus attention separates perceptual figure from perceptual noise or background (Kahneman 1973, Treisman 1969). Selectivity is the defining characteristic of attention and this suggests that attention is a major cognitive process involved in selective thinking.

When people try to find solutions to problems they concentrate on some aspects of problem situations and ignore others of lesser interest. Attention enables people to perceive the stimulus environment in a differentiated manner. While object perception, for example, deals with form, colour, depth and movement, attention divides the perceived stimulus environment into preferred and non-preferred parts (Allport 1989, Gibson 1986, Marr 1982, Rock 1983, Uhlman 1984, van der Heijden 1990). This property of attention makes it much more important than object perception, when thinking is considered. The elements of a problem very seldom, if ever, stand alone without any background information. If the elements are objects or deeds; they are among other objects and deeds; that is, among background information. The noise makes the preferences unavoidable, because thinking must be related to the relevant parts of environment. Hence, thinking requires attention. Without attentive processes orientation to the environment would be impossible and without orienting ourselves we cannot think.

Several famous phenomena in the psychology of thinking are evidently linked with attention. Fixation, set, insight, Bartlett's (1958) point-of-no-return and action slips may serve as typical examples (Duncker 1945, Köhler 1917/1957, Luchins 1942, Maier 1930, 1931, Norman 1981, Wertheimer 1945). In all these phenomena the elements of the situation are fully visible, but the preferences in encoding divide the stimulus environment into more and less relevant parts with various intriguing consequences. The preferences among stimuli, which are prerequisites for these phenomena, are impossible without selective perception and thus attention is an important component in them.

Both intuition and tradition support the relevance of attentional processes for thinking, but still very little concrete research can be found. Very seldom has anyone tried to splice together these two theoretical notions, attention and thinking. Even though in expertise research, for example, well-argued connections between memory and thinking have long been established, only a few researchers have been interested in the relationship between attention and thinking (for example, cf. Ericsson and Smith 1991, Gilhooly and Green 1992). For the want of empirical data even the best current reviews on thinking and expertise do not have much to say about the role of attention in thinking.

The problem of analysing the links between attention and thinking can hardly be methodological. The connection between memory and thinking is no more direct and yet plenty of research into memory and thinking can be found (Ericsson and Smith 1991, Gilhooly and Green 1992). There is absolutely no reason why procedures analogous to those that have been used in studying the relationship between thinking and memory could not be adopted when studying the possible links between attention and thinking. As has been done in memory and thinking research, expertise effects on attention and thinking can be compared (Chase and Simon 1973a, b). Thus no objective reason can be found to justify the relatively modest interest in the role of attention in thinking. The neglect of this issue may, then, be an accident of fashion.

Attention has several attributes that presumably are linked with thought processes. Because of the lack of empirical evidence, it is not possible to consider all relevant attributes, but enough is known about the main features of attention and attentional changes with chess expertise that the main features of the connections can be considered. For example, it would be good to know something about vigilance in chess, but at the moment this is not possible. Consequently, I shall concentrate on basic capacity, perceptual learning and automatization, on the nature of attentional processes and representations and the main characteristics of voluntary attending.

CAPACITY OF ATTENTION

The basic capacity of attention is one unit, unless a task is highly automatized (Allport 1980a, b, Broadbent 1958, James 1890, Kahneman 1973, Norman and Bobrow 1975, Schneider *et al.* 1984, Treisman 1969, van der Heijden 1990; for recent reviews see Allport 1989, Shiffrin 1988, van der Heijden 1990). Under some conditions people can carry out two or even more simultaneous tasks. However, when overlapping processing resources are needed the dual task performance is mostly very difficult, if not impossible (Allport 1979, 1980a, b, Allport *et al.* 1972, Heuer and Wing 1984, Shaffer 1975).

The limits of attentional capacity raise several questions concerning attention and thinking in chess. Chess players are experts. Could it be that their attentional capacity has improved in the course of many years of training? Could this improved capacity explain skill differences in chess, which in the end are differences in the ability to think? Could it be that improved selective perception provides an explanation for improved selective thinking? On the other hand, if the speculation of improved attentional capacity proves to be wrong, what can selective attention explain about selective thinking? Surely, the answers must be sought by analysing the existing empirical data.

Djakov *et al.* (1926) were the first researchers to document an interest in attentional processes in chess. They wished to know whether chess players are attentionally supernormal. If expertise in chess improved the attentional capacity of chess players, this would be an important clue in trying to understand the skill of expert chess players. The data they provided suggested a negative answer to their question. They failed to find any attentional superiority of chess players in any of their attentional subtasks, and the 'psychogram' of chess players was practically identical to that of laymen (Djakov *et al.* 1926). Thus, it seems logical to conclude that chess players' basic attentional capacity is normal and also that chess training cannot change this capacity.

Nothing in later research has suggested that Djakov *et al.* (1926) were wrong, and thus we can fairly safely conclude that chess training does not improve the basic capacity of attention. Chess masters, like everyone else, can attend to just one thing at a time. This is undoubtedly an important piece of information, since it explains why chess players' thinking must be selective.

The basic limits of attentional capacity suggest that expert chess players cannot attend to more than one thing simultaneously, and, hence, the players cannot think about more than one solution hypothesis at the time. De Groot's (1965) empirical data very strongly support this conclusion. In none of his reported protocols did subjects relate more than one set of logically connected moves at one time. Hence, the capacity of attention forces thinking to select. We can perceive objects in just one way at a time, not in two or three different ways. To think actively and concurrently about two continuations in a game would overload the attentional system, because two different representations would have to be kept in consciousness at the same time. This would certainly require over-lapping resources, because we do not have resources to build two simultaneous and contradictory representations. Ambiguous figures such as Necker's cube might serve as an example (Rock 1983). Consequently, thinking is bound to attentional capacity.

LOW-LEVEL PERCEPTUAL LEARNING

Though the basic capacity of human attention is very limited, it does not mean that our performance in attentional tasks is necessarily unaffected by any training. People learn to perceive things (Gibson 1969). Capacity refers to the number of things we can attend to at a time but says nothing about the speed or accuracy with which we can attend. Capacity tells us very little about the time sharing and other means by which people try to circumvent basic attentional limitations. This means that perceptual learning must be considered separately, since any improvement or disintegration in attentional performance should be reflected in thinking. Improved efficiency on one processing level must have consequences in a process such as thinking, which actively occupies each available information processing resource.

One deficiency in the work of Djakov *et al.* (1926) was that they used only general attentional tasks. Thus their early research does not provide any information about the changes in chess-specific performance as a consequence of expertise. The possible improvement in chess-specific attentional tasks was studied much later by Saariluoma (1984, 1985, 1990a). He was interested in the distribution of expertise in the information processing system. Would it begin with visual feature systems or would the standard chess patterns in memory be the first level of expertise?

Saariluoma (1984, 1985, 1990a) used chess-specific perceptual classification tasks to measure the changes in visual attention caused by increased expertise. Perceptual classification tasks comprise tasks in which subjects divide presented objects into target and the background. Visual search is probably the most important task of this class, but it can be varied in several ways and thus the term perceptual classification is appropriate here (for discussions of visual search tasks see Neisser 1963, 1967, Rabbitt 1978, 1984, Shiffrin 1988).

The first task was termed the selective enumeration task. In this task subjects were instructed to count the number of minor pieces, i.e. bishops and knights, in real and in random positions. In this way two hypotheses could be tested: first, are experts faster than novices in discriminating target pieces, and second, does randomization of positions destroy the possible effects of skill? The latter question is important because random positions do not have any chess-specific sense. If the skilled subjects suffer more than novices from the randomization, it means that the positions are processed up to the system of chess-specific relations. Experts can benefit from their better knowledge of these relations in game positions but in random positions they cannot similarly gain advantage from their chess-specific knowledge (Chase and Simon 1973a, b). On the other hand, if randomization does not cause any skill-related impairment, it strongly suggests that stimulus processing remains on a low, feature level in these basic attentional tasks and that skill differences in processing chess positions begin on the level of feature analysis.

The experiments systematically supported the last alternative (see Figure 3.1). In selective enumeration experiments skilled subjects are faster than less skilled subjects and skilled subjects are superior

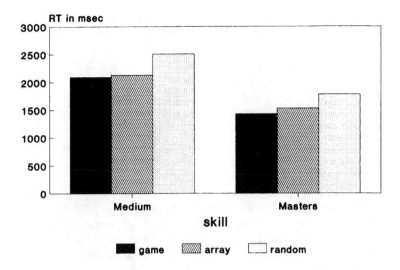

Figure 3.1 Chess players' reaction time (RT) latencies in an enumeration task in game positions, array positions (i.e. positions in which all the pieces are placed side by side in the form of an array) and random positions. Players of master and medium strength were shown positions of the three types and asked to count as rapidly as possible the number of bishops and knights on the board

even when positions are randomized (Saariluoma 1984, 1985). Even when all pieces are laid side by side in arrays, stimuli are processed faster by experts (Saariluoma 1990a). Usually the random–game difference is additive, suggesting that this difference in reaction times is caused by differences in the surface layouts between game and random positions (Saariluoma 1984). In game positions pieces are organized into groups with the same colours, which is not the case in random positions, and the locations of pieces are much more predictable in game than in random positions. Both are factors that should affect search speed through figural synthesis (see, for example, Kahneman 1973).

Further information about the locus of skill in perceptual organization can be found by adding total enumeration conditions to the previous design. In total enumeration subjects count not just the number of minor pieces, but the total number of pieces on the board (Saariluoma 1990a). The difference in task demands between total and selective enumeration is clear. In selective enumeration subjects must segregate the target pieces from all the other pieces, but in total enumeration this is unnecessary. It is sufficient that they discriminate a piece as an object from the non-object background. The system of discriminative cues is very different in the two cases, and consequently if skill is located at the feature discrimination level, skill effects should disappear in total enumeration, because everybody can discriminate an object against an empty background. Moreover, differences between game and random conditions should diminish, because discrimination is not needed and thus the predictability of the locations or colour areas should not be important. The two predictions were also verified in an experiment by Saariluoma (1990a).

The normal skill difference could be found in selective enumeration but, surprisingly, this difference disappeared in total enumeration (see Figure 3.2). Moreover, in total enumeration random positions were slightly easier than the game positions, while in selective enumeration the difference between random and game positions was clear and reversed.

The comparison between selective and total enumeration implies that the skill differences originate in the learned discriminative feature systems. The differences in the feature systems explain

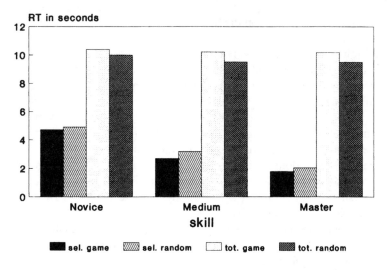

Figure 3.2 Master, medium-strength and novice chess players' RT latencies in selective and total enumeration. In selective enumeration the players counted the number of knights and bishops on the board and in total enumeration they counted all the pieces

experts' superiority in piece detection and enumeration tasks. Experts know better than novices how to discriminate a bishop from the other pieces, but the difference practically disappears when subjects must discriminate a bishop against an empty background (Saariluoma 1984, 1990a). This is possible only if processing superiority is associated with discriminative features. This explains also the disappearance of the position type effect. The positions themselves are not visually different, but the search for particular pieces is much more difficult in random positions.

Skill differences begin with the knowledge of discriminative features. The discriminative feature hypothesis has also been the major explanation for perceptual learning (Gibson 1969, La Berge 1976, Neisser 1963, 1967, Shiffrin 1988). People learn to process familiar perceptual stimulus classes faster by learning to discriminate the crucial features and by learning to build functional combinations of these features (La Berge 1976, Navon 1989a,b). Thus the idea that chess expertise begins with feature discrimination seems to fit well with what we know about visual attention and perceptual learning (e.g. Gibson 1969, Kahneman 1973).

The improvement of discriminative feature processing as a consequence of training is a sign that chess players' conceptual structures are distributed. Conceptual knowledge in the chess mind begins with the very low-level feature discrimination systems. Undoubtedly, the ability to discriminate pieces swiftly also helps chess players in stimulus processing. It may even explain some lapses of attention and increased speed in processing more complex targets, such as threats and mates. Yet these attentional results explain very little about thinking itself. Thinking is not simply object discrimination, and discriminative features do not belong to the conscious contents of chess players' thinking.

Perhaps the most interesting conclusion concerns human conceptual system. Chess skill is a learned skill and no one has a biological processing system for chess. This means that the effects of training can be seen in human ability to categorize the environment. This categorization ability is partly stored in unconscious and preconceptual cognitive units such as the systems of discriminative features.

MENTAL TRANSFORMATION AND HIGH-LEVEL PERCEPTUAL PROCESSING

The counting of minor pieces is one of the simplest chess-specific perceptual tasks since pieces form the lowest level of chess-specific information. It is far from the kind of processes that are central in thinking. Much closer are the tasks in which moves are targets, because the 'noticing' or detection of moves is a necessary subtask in chess players' thinking.

Moves and move sequences demand more complicated processing than piece detection. As it is illegal to move the pieces when thinking, chess players must mentally transform them from one square to another to represent a move in their mind (Chase and Simon 1973a, b, Church and Church 1977, Milojkovic 1982). Hence the next step in investigation of chess players' perceptual selection is to test the validity and generalizability of the basic enumeration results in move detection tasks.

The detection of moves is necessary in chess. If chess players do not notice the threats before it is too late, they will lose. Chess depends on small things. Losing a pawn in an uncontrolled way usually leads at the master level to a forced loss of the game. Therefore, in high-level chess momentary lapses of attention should not occur. A minor error easily leads to the waste of hours of work (Saariluoma 1984, 1992b). Consequently, it is logical to assume that expert chess players are better at noticing threats. This being so, a part of their superiority in thinking has also been discovered.

The simplest task for testing the assumption about experts' superiority in noticing threats takes place on an otherwise empty board. Saariluoma (1984) carried out one such experiment to see whether experts are superior to novices in noticing simple threats. In this experiment subjects were asked to decide as fast as possible whether the king was in check or not when there were only two pieces on the board. The skill differences between the subjects in this experiment were made as large as possible. The strongest participant was one of the world's top-level grandmasters with a rating of around 2,600 ELO points and the weakest subjects were novices with practically no experience of chess at all. In addition, some experts with ratings around 2,000 points and novices with some experience of school chess but with no rating were studied. Despite these large differ-

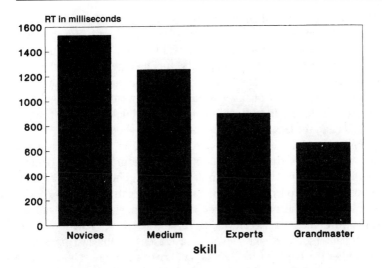

RT in milliseconds

Figure 3.3 The RT latencies of chess players of four different strengths in check detection tasks, without background pieces. Subjects were presented with chessboards on which were two pieces – king and some opposite-colour major piece – and were asked to decide as rapidly as possible whether the king was in check or not

ences in skill, the reaction times differed by a little less than one second (see Figure 3.3).

Piece discrimination is not the only source of skill differences in check detection tasks. The encoding of spatial threat relations between the king and the checking piece also causes skill-related differences. This conclusion is emphasized by the fact that the measured skill differences in the detection of a single piece on an empty board were around 60 milliseconds but in the detection of check the differences were much larger (Saariluoma 1984). The results suggest that chess players learn not only to discriminate pieces but also to make the required mental transformations faster. In this task subjects need not really discriminate pieces from anything other than an empty background. This means that the skill difference is almost totally accounted for by looking to see whether the target and background pieces are correctly located.

The results of the check detection task without background pieces cannot be directly generalized to check detection when other pieces are present in the background. The crucial problem is whether the check is detected by serial comparisons, or whether it is detected directly. Assuming that detection is based on serial comparison, such that subjects look at each possible piece until they find the right one, latencies in reaction time (RT) should show a number of characteristics. First, they should be much larger than in the previous experiment, because subjects must compare on average ten pieces to discover a positive instance, and twenty to respond to a negative instance. Indeed, RTs for masters should be from 5 to 10 seconds and for less experienced players they should be well over 10 seconds. In this case no piece discrimination time is assumed. Second, the RTs should be roughly the same in game and random conditions. Only the discrimination time should be different between the two conditions. Finally, the negative response times should be around twice as large as for the positive trials, and the skill differences between negative and positive reaction times should interact with skill level. The reason for the last prediction is simple: the twenty successive comparisons that are required for a negative decision should take twice as much time as should the ten comparisons required for a positive decision. If one comparison takes more time from novices than experts, this should cause an interaction between skill and the type of decision. If this schema

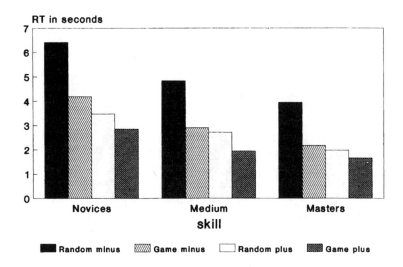

Figure 3.4 Chess players' performance in a check detection task. The subject had to decide whether either king was in check or not in game and random positions with over twenty pieces on the board

fails it means that check detection is very probably parallel and that a check is treated as a holistic pattern.

Saariluoma (1984, 1985) conducted experiments on check detection to test the generalizability of the minor piece counting results in the visual search of complex chess-specific targets. In the experiments subjects were instructed to say as quickly as possible whether a king was in check or not. This was done both in game and in random positions. Accordingly, four reaction time parameters could be measured: game and check, game and no-check, random and check, and finally random and no check. The results (see Figure 3.4) were analogous with the main findings of the minor piece counting experiments, and falsified the serial comparison assumption. Experts were faster than the less experienced subjects but the overall reaction times were much smaller than one would predict on the grounds of a simple serial comparison. The differences between the four conditions had an additive character. However, random negative trials took more time than game negative trials, but no skill-related interaction was found. Hence, the differences between conditions depended more on the properties of the stimuli than on the level of skill.

Threats are necessary elements in chess players' thinking. Overlooking one threat may mean the loss of the game. This means that chess players must have a system of 'threat detectors' that call their attention to any threat. These threat detectors must be learned patterns that are activated when necessary. It is clear that thinking very strongly depends on the threat detectors. If they do not warn subjects about dangers, even the most beautiful and elegant combinations are just a waste of time. This means that the analysis of a position depends on noticing very elementary features. Presumably, this kind of connection between attention and thought is not chess-specific, but experts must always be alert for possible critical factors in the stimulus when trying to find a solution. Think, for example, how much extra work small and innocent-looking lapses of attention cause in computer programming.

ATTENDING TO COMPLEX PATTERNS

Assuming that chess players learn increasingly more complex patterns as their expertise increases, one might expect that when the complexity of a task increases the skill differences also become proportionally larger. Expert chess players have their task-specific

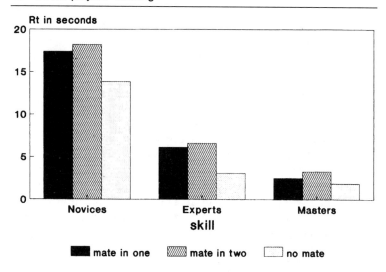

Figure 3.5 One-move mate task in three sets of circumstances: a one-move mate was possible; no mate was possible; or the subject had to decide as rapidly as possible whether he or she could mate the opponent's king

processing patterns and they can use them even more effectively when more processing is required to carry out the task. Saariluoma (1984) asked subjects at different levels to say as fast as possible whether White could checkmate in one move. Two control conditions were used. In the first no mate was possible and in the second only a two-move mate was possible.

The skill differences in RT latencies were much larger than in any of the above experiments. The complexity of the task made the reaction times longer. Interestingly, the no-mate conditions were the fastest and the two-move mate the slowest. This suggests that the differences between the conditions were caused by the micro search and inference processes. These processes were used to make sure that the decision was correct. In no-mate conditions a player must know only that the king is not in check; in mate-in-one conditions subjects must find whether the king is in check and has no escape. In mate-in-two conditions subjects must decide whether an escape is possible. Thus, the mate-in-two conditions were the most difficult, as can be seen in the reaction times (Figure 3.5). They were the most difficult because they involved the largest number of threat and defence relationships that had to be detected (Saariluoma 1984).

The speed and accuracy of experts show that they have learned complex representations that they can use in detecting checkmates. A checkmate can be found in a controlled manner by first looking to see whether a piece is checking the king and thereafter whether the king has an escape route. The difference between skill groups is, however, so large that experts' processing must be highly automatized. Undoubtedly, recognition-type mechanisms as discussed by Chase and Simon (1973b) are actively used to decrease the processing time and errors.

The results show also that check detection is not simple template matching, but requires automatic processes to verify the proposed sequence of moves. If processing had been a template matching type single process, the difference between control conditions would not show the necessity of micro-search processes. Obviously, chess players first get some idea about the possible mate and then verify whether the situation really is a mate. The examination is more time consuming with two-move mates than in situations where no mate is possible.

Perceptual learning develops in subprocesses in chess players' minds, and these subprocesses speed up the actual problem-solving process. Thus thinking is partly built on the learned content of specific modules, such as standard moves, mating patterns, etc. It can be assumed that these modules can be freely coupled to carry out an attentional task (cf. Allport 1980a, b, Navon 1989a, b).

A one-move mate task is, of course, very close to real problem solving in content. Normally, two-move mates can produce highly demanding problems. Though the current tasks were not really problematic they illustrate the connection between attentional modules and selective thinking. Expertise in selective thinking is, partly at least, built on these attentional modules. They focus expert players' attention and they provide useful subroutines for processing.

AUTOMATIZATION

Experts have developed well-learned routines or task-specific modules for processing chess-specific stimuli. The next problem concerns the development of the modules. How do chess players learn these chess-specific processing units? The standard explanation would be automatization. When the moves and mating patterns are repeated sufficiently often in consistent conditions, the attentional modules should evolve in chess players' minds.

The previous experiments do not, however, directly test this explanation; it is merely a logical assumption. To test the automatization explanation properly, one should construct an experiment in which controlled processing is changed into automatic processing by consistent mapping and the results should be compared with the above experiments.

Fisk and Lloyd (1988) decided to conduct such an experiment. They had novice subjects who were tested under consistent mapping conditions. They showed their subjects a board on which there were six upper-case letters plus a flashing target T. Their task was to decide which one of the characters could take the target. Consistency of mapping meant simply that each letter was always mapped with the same piece movement rule.

The results show how consistent mapping very effectively and very rapidly decreases the RT latencies. After a few hours a corresponding speed was achieved that in normal chess training would take three to four years. However, an asymptote was reached and no further improvement could be demonstrated (see Figure 3.6). To approach even closer to the experts' level further training was necessary. Nevertheless, the experiment demonstrated very directly the connection between automatization and skill differences in chess-specific perceptual classification. As a consequence of automatization the number of errors decreases, the speed of performance

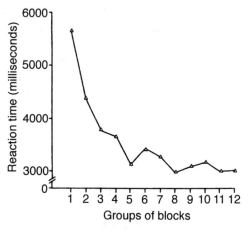

Figure 3.6 Results of Fisk and Lloyd (1988) in automatization task

increases, and the required cognitive load becomes smaller. Often the processing acquires unconscious characteristics and the capacity demands greatly decrease (Neumann 1984, 1990, Schneider *et al.* 1984, Shiffrin 1988). All these consequences can be found in expert chess players' attentional modules. However, only in the laboratory have they been produced under consistent mapping conditions.

Chess players learn the task-specific modules by playing and training on chess. They study games from books or computer databases but they do not normally use consistent training. Yet over a period of a few years they develop a large store of auto-matized, chess-specific modules. This means that years of varied-mapping training may cause analogous effects to consistent training in laboratory. The time needed is just much longer. This is a point that would benefit from more research.

VOLUNTARY ATTENTION

The previous sections have shown that skill in chess strongly correlates with a high level of performance in chess-specific per-ceptual classification tasks. Chess players' cognitive capacity or the resources in perceptual classification increase with training. How-ever, the connection between these results and thinking is in no way straightforward. Though our attentional capacity is one unit at a time, a thinking person can pay attention to several different objects during several minutes of thought processes. All kinds of informa-tion can be gathered and collected. This means that to understand the connections between attention and thinking we should first understand voluntary attending.

In all the experiments discussed so far, the experimenter has defined the target or the target class to the subjects. This is not the case in chess players' selective thinking. They are free to attend to what they wish. Real-life attentional selection is thus voluntary and we must analyse voluntary attending in order to understand the logic of module coupling and the scope and limits of selective attention as explanations of selective thinking.

Eye movements of chess players provide some clues about the nature of voluntary information gathering during chess players' problem solving. These studies were set up to show that chess players' vision is highly selective. The scanpaths are not distributed equally over the squares of a chessboard but instead concentrate on some areas which are vital for ongoing thought (Tikhomirov 1988,

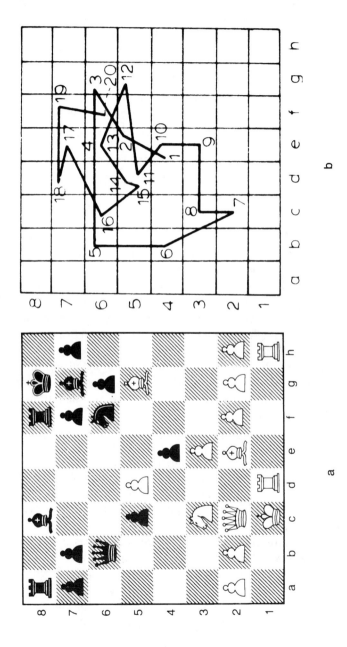

Figure 3.7 Eye movement registrations by Tikhomirov and Poznyanskaya (1966)

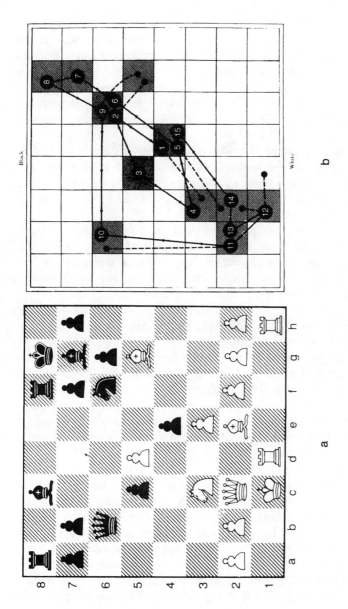

Figure 3.8 PERCEIVER's simulation of eye movements in Tikhomirov and Poznyanskaya's (1966) position
Source: Simon and Barenfeld (1969)

Tikhomirov and Poznyanskaya 1966; similar data were also obtained by Charness and Reingold 1992).

Tikhomirov and Poznyanskaya (1966) reported several properties of eye movements. They found that the number of fixations increased linearly as the presentation time increased. The scan paths formed a repeating cycle on the most vital squares and pieces, and therefore they seemed to concentrate on the most informative areas of the board (Figure 3.7). Finally, the eyes often followed some hypothetical possibilities, i.e. moves which were never made, but which had to be taken into account in searching for the best move (Tikhomirov 1988, Tikhomirov and Poznyanskaya 1966).

Simon and Barenfeld (1969) went further in this direction. They argued that the eyes follow threat and defence relationships in a position. They also wrote a computer simulation program to support their argument and called this program PERCEIVER. PERCEIVER's eye paths are presented in Figure 3.8.

The surprising similarity between the real and the simulated scanpaths support Simon and Barenfeld's (1969) argument. Just by assuming a very simple heuristic based on threat and defence relationships, it is possible to achieve a selectivity that is close to human eye movements.

There is one very evident difference between Tikhomirov and Poznyanskaya's (1966) and Simon and Barenfeld's (1969) analysis. In real eye movement data, fixations are often focused on the empty squares. This is true for the Tikhomirov and Poznyanskaya (1966) study as well as in the Charness and Reingold (1992) data. In addition, Reynolds (1982) pointed out that the attention of chess players is focused on empty squares which form a zone of orientation (see also Tikhomirov and Poznyanskaya 1966). The scope of the simulation should thus be improved to incorporate the whole zone of orientation.

Before it is possible to consider a simulation of the whole zone of orientation an explanation must be found for this centralized attention. Holding (1985, 1992a) made the first step forward by suggesting that the trajectories of the pieces or 'powerlines' should be taken into account. This hypothesis can be further elaborated by studying the possible information content of the empty squares.

A careful look at the registered eye movements shows that eye movements follow both real and hypothetical moves. An example is given in Tikhomirov and Poznyanskaya (1966) (see the position in

Figures 3.7 and 3.8), where Black intends to play his or her bishop to f5. The eyes search for White playing the imaginary move g4, which is supported by the bishop on e2, in order to chase the f5 bishop to d7. In this way fixations on three, possibly four empty squares can be explained with one variation. The counter-arguments do not refute Simon and Barenfeld's (1969) idea that threat and defence relations may play an important part in chess players' thinking, and that search relies on threats and defences even when moves are imaginary. However, the explanation for fixations on the empty squares made so far are speculative and more research is needed to improve our understanding of functions of the eye movements in chess players' information intake.

One reason for the importance of threat and defence structures can be found by studying errors (Saariluoma 1992b). As already pointed out, missing one trivial threat may render hours of work futile. Indeed, very skilled chess players seldom make this kind of blunder, though they are common in the games of novices (Saari-luoma 1984, 1992b, see also Chapter 6). Threats are important and the interpretation made by Simon and Barenfeld (1969) fits thus very nicely with the general conviction that the eye movements concentrate on the informative and important areas of a stimulus (Mackworth and Morandi 1966, Yarbus 1967).

Further support for the previous results on perceptual selectivity can be found by using a slightly different method. Tikhomirov and Terehov (1969) decided to study blind chess players with a technique they termed the cyclographic method. By this they meant the registration of the tactual hand movements of subjects. This is a very good idea because blind chess players normally examine a chess position tactually, and in this way the experiments reached a very high level of ecological validity. In their experiments Tikhomirov and Terehov (1969) found a highly selective pattern of tactual movements which was remarkably similar to the selective scan-paths. An example is presented in Figure 3.9.

Tikhomirov and Terehov (1969) argued that the search path of blind chess players is repetitive and gradually converges. The number of elements studied, i.e. the number of squares, decreases when the search time increases (Tikhomirov 1988). Perhaps the subjects' search slowly transforms from search to verification and this causes the convergence (Tikhomirov 1988). It is unfortunately not possible to draw any further conclusions since the empirical data concerning chess players' eye and hand movements are still rela-

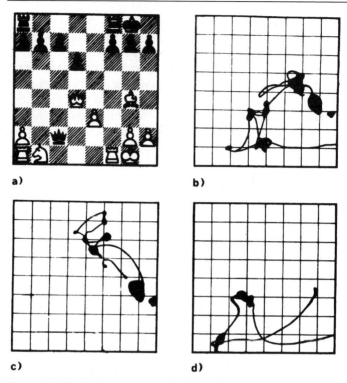

a)   b)

c)   d)

Figure 3.9 Tactual movements by blind chess players
Source: Tikhomirov (1975)

tively sparse and eye movements have proved to be elusive. More-over, so far the types of positions have not been varied system-atically, which prevents a more detailed examination. The same is also true with blind chess players' hand movements. However, the current evidence demonstrates the selectivity of chess players' information processing and the importance of threat and defence relationships.

ATTENTION IN CHESS

The basic attentional capacity of chess players is one unit, as it is with all people. Chess training does not improve this capacity. Non-chess-specific attentional tests show this very clearly. It can also be indirectly seen in the additivity of stimulus-type effects. If expertise had the effect of changing all attentional limits no such systematic additivity should be found.

Despite the basic capacity limitations, many years of systematic training greatly improves expert chess players' performance in chess-based attentional tasks. Their speed and accuracy is superior to that of novices. This improvement is caused by an automatization, like that for perceptual learning process. Chess players have learned attentional processing modules that can be coupled freely to find optimal performance (cf. Allport 1980a, b, Navon 1989a, b).

Chess players' attentional processing seems thus to be limited by the task structure and expertise. The notion of data and resource limitations describes effectively the contrary effects of capacity and perceptual learning (Norman and Bobrow 1975). Because attentional capacity is unaffected by skill, changes in task demands and stimulus type affect all skill groups in a similar way. However, those aspects of processing which require discrimination of the stimulus or faster mental transformations seem to change with improvements in the relevant cognitive skills.

Attentional chess expertise is thus achieved by developing modular task-specific units that contain both discrimination and transformation components. Discrimination begins with the visual features and ends with complex piece configurations and move patterns. Since these modules are automatized they save both time and processing capacity for other subtasks that are necessary during problem solving.

The attentional modules control voluntary attention in several ways. They call attention to critical points in a chess position. Threats, for example, are detected by these automatized models. The activated modules also direct attention to the relevant areas on the chessboard and thus keep a player attending to important features of the game.

ATTENTION AND SELECTIVE THINKING

Apparently, attentional selectivity explains all information selection that is needed in selective thinking. Attentional modules control voluntary attending and focus the gaze on the relevant chess-specific issues. Attention filters irrelevant information from representations and thus keeps them concentrating on relevant information content. Though logical, this model is anything but complete and indeed selectivity in thinking cannot be reduced to its subservient, attentional selectivity.

The first problem concerns what is actually attended to when trying to find a good move. The eye movements show that subjects' voluntary attention concentrates, for example, on threat and defence relationships or moves (Simon and Barenfeld 1969, Tikhomirov 1988). But in what sense can we attend to a threat or a series of moves? Neither of them are present in the visual stimulus. A chess player just imagines the moves and superimposes the image on the chessboard. What the eyes follow in voluntary attention does not exist in the stimulus. The function of the stimulus is to work as an external memory, or notepad, which assists mental transformations.

Yet chess players' eye movements follow the correct series of locations for the imagined moves. This means that the representation has two superimposed levels. The first level is the actual physical board, to which a chess player is actively attending in order to find a good move. This representation could be generated by anyone. Even a person without any chess-specific knowledge can attend to any location on a chessboard. The second representational level is chess specific. On this level the board is superimposed with moves, combinations of moves, weak points, patterns, etc. No one but a strong chess player can represent the board in this way and the questions of content-specific relevance, for example, belong to this representational level.

The second level is generated on the basis of the first level. What precise form the second-level representation takes depends on the precise position. Errors in encoding the first level – for example, confusing a bishop with a queen – affect the second-level representation. On the other hand the physical locations that are relevant and to which the player should direct his or her gaze depend on the second-level representation.

The big conceptual problem with the two representational levels is which of the two levels chess players attend to when they look at a chessboard. I would argue for the first level, and I shall later suggest that we must postulate new theoretical concepts to study the second representational level. Only by limiting attention to selecting perceptual information may we keep the conceptual system of cognitive psychology sufficiently analytical with respect to these two representational levels.

In fact, the idea of two representational levels is not chess-specific. If we think of language comprehension, two very similar representational levels are apparent. On the one hand, we have physical sentences, spoken or written, and on the other we have their meanings. I find it natural to say that we attend to physical words and sentences, but I find it very hard to understand what it would mean to be attending to sentence meanings. It is even natural to say that someone attends to sentences with certain meanings, but this does not mean that that person is attending to their meanings. The reason is simple: we construct the meanings of the sentences on the grounds of logic and information stored in memory, which is linked to physical sentences. The physical sentences must be semantically interpreted before their meaning can be presented and the processes needed in semant interpretation are no longer attentional processes. In an analogous way, the construction of the second-level representation of a chessboard requires selective processes which go beyond attention.

The problems with the two representational levels stem from the current concept of attention. Evidently, these problems have been noticed by attention researchers, who over the years have been worried about the absence of content in attentional information processing (e.g. Allport 1980a, b, van der Heijden 1990). Attention is a process that selects the figure in perceptual information. It is said that attention is directed towards some aspect of the stimulus environment. Here, the directing mechanisms, an 'attentional supervisor', an 'anarchistic coupling system' or whatever, does not make any difference (Navon 1989a,b, Norman and Shallice 1986). The main thing is that attention directs gaze to some aspect of the physical stimulus enviroment and selects the figure of the perceptual stimulus.

Attention is directed to something. It tries to pick up some information. However, attention does not define what is relevant information. It just finds the information. Allport (1989) argued that attention operates on 'what' and 'where'. The important thing to understand here is that what 'what' is, is not an attentional question. Attentional research and attention itself presuppose the contents of 'what' and do not define it. Attention provides us with the knowledge where the 'what' is, assuming it is present at all.

It would be possible to refine and sharpen the notion of attention so that semantic interpretation of the physical world fell within its rubric, but this would be pointless for several reasons. It would reduce the analytical power of cognitive jargon by classifying very different phenomena under one and the same notions. The most important attributes of attention such as capacity or location are not very efficient in expressing contents. They simply do not have suitable attributes.

Even more important is to understand that the semantic representation, which defines the goal for attentional system, need not have any physical stimulus at all. It is not stimulus-bound like attention. We can easily represent the physically non-present future or past. We can represent the road behind a hillock though we could not attend to it. We can represent on the semantic level complex objects such as society, universe, infinity, atom. However, we cannot attend to any of these, except in a metaphorical sense.

Attentional selectivity cannot thus explain the content-specific selectivity required in selective thinking. It cannot tell us what are the chess-specific issues that are important for the good conduct of a chess game. A new content-specific selection process must be postulated in order to study content-specific selection. Attention research can merely provide information about the existence of the targets and their locations. The meaning and sense of the targets is beyond attention.

Chapter 4

Memory capacity

Selective information processing in thinking cannot be reduced to attentional selectivity. The contents of representations which are not stimulus-bound are not explainable using attentional concepts. A very natural subsequent question is whether memory could provide such a set of attributes that would allow it to deal with content specific selectivity. Because memory is needed in associating stimulus information with all task-specific knowledge in the expert's mind, the explanatory power of memory looks much more promising than was the explanatory power of attention.

The connections between memory and thinking have been widely acknowledged (Anderson 1976, 1983, Ericsson and Kintsch 1994). Of course, memory is a necessary component in thinking. Human thoughts cannot be stored when there is nothing to manipulate, and thus memory is the platform for the representation of thoughts. All thoughts must all the time be in working memory or in long-term memory and thus the limits of memory necessarily dictate some limits for thoughts. Thoughts cannot contain what memory cannot represent.

The information processing in memory systems has its specific organization and this organization must maintain thinking and endorse the selectivity. Memory is a precondition of thinking and thus it is a precondition for the very possibility of selective thinking. Thus it would seem reasonable to suggest that information selection in thinking could be expressed in terms of memory processes. Hence, in the continuation of this thesis, the chess memory literature will be reviewed in order to assess how much of chess players' selective thinking can be explained in terms of memory. This is an empirical question and thus it requires specific experimental information about the way chess players' memory systems operate.

When we understand the principles of memory, we shall be in a much better position in all our attempts to consider what in selective thinking is caused by the structure and operation of memory.

RECOGNITION MEMORY

Recognition has been argued to be essential in selective thinking. Numerous researchers since Thomas Hobbes (1651) have suggested that people recognize familiar ideas in new situations, and consequently they are able to discover good ideas. Recognition activates hypothetical solutions in the minds of chess players, and experts differ from novices with respect to the ability to recognize better base moves (Calderwood *et al.* 1988, Chase and Simon 1973a, b, de Groot 1965, 1966, Klein 1989, Klein and Peio 1989). Experts have accumulated a vast knowledge base of piece and move configurations and this increases their chances of generating a good hypothesis. The recognition process selects the ideas that are implemented from among all the ideas that are available, and thus selective thinking is basically recognition.

Surprising as it may seem, very little empirical evidence has been published concerning recognition in chess. If recognition is one of the most important subprocesses in selective thinking, as has been argued, one would expect to find a great deal of empirical material on recognition, but this is not the case. The neglect of recognition means that we have underestimated the complexity of recognition, and we cannot justify the assumption that the contribution from recognition is clear-cut. Perhaps the weight of tradition has prevented us from analysing this concept critically, which is as much a problem for as an explanation for selectivity in thinking.

The only empirically analysed problem in the literature is the test of expert v. novice differences in recognition memory. Do these differences really account for experts' superiority as compared with novices in recognizing chess positions? Even although recognition is often seen as a very effective cognitive process, the empirical results of recognition experiments may vary widely. Hence it is not clear what recognition can explain of selective thinking.

The human capacity to store and recognize pictorial information is almost unlimited. Standing (1973) showed 10,000 everyday pictures to people and noticed that they were able to recognize about 90 per cent of them. The results were dramatic, but some other types of recognition experiments may provide very different outcomes. If the difference between presented pictures and distractors is very small, recognition may be virtually guesswork (e.g. Mandler and Parker 1976).

In recognition experiments with chess players a new factor, skill, appears and a researcher must account for skill-dependent variation. What is easy for experts is impossible for novices. Goldin (1978b, 1979) conducted some recognition memory experiments. In one of the experiments she presented her subjects with twenty-one stimulus positions and gave them a block visualization test. This was followed by a test of recognition involving multiple target distractor pairs. The recognition percentage was high, and subjects with United States Chess Federation (USCF) ratings from 800 to about 1,986 scored on average 87.6 per cent correct. The results showed also that the recall percentage was closely related to chess skill. The more skilled a player the better the recognition percentage (Goldin 1978b).

In another experiment Goldin (1978b) used eighty real and eighty scrambled positions. Subjects were presented with forty real and forty random positions and afterwards their ability to select stimulus positions correctly from stimulus distractor pairs was compared.

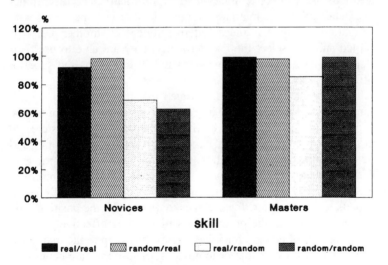

Figure 4.1 Recognition in chess. Subjects of two ability levels had to recognize chess positions they had seen earlier under four different stimulus distractor conditions
Source: Goldin (1978b)

Skill differences were clear in Goldin's (1978b) experiment (see Figure 4.1), and the overall performance was again high. Interestingly, the recognition of random positions was also good.

Saariluoma (1984) used a yes–no recognition test and obtained very similar results to Goldin (1978b). He presented his subjects first with thirty real and thirty random positions and then positions were shuffled among sixty new game and random positions. The skill difference was very high in both conditions, though the game positions were better recognized by all skill groups. The results of recognition experiments show how the well-known difference between recognition and recall is valid in chess. People are able to recognize pictorial materials very effectively if the differences in materials are sufficiently large (Shepard 1967, Standing 1973). The chess positions seem to be very easily discriminated by experts, but novices have great difficulties (Saariluoma 1984). This means that pre-learned chess-specific patterns increase the ability to discriminate positions.

The superiority of the experts remains in random conditions. This is probably due to selective stimulus processing. In recall tests subjects must reproduce all the pieces, but in recognizing random positions one can concentrate on some informative and discriminative details. Subjects may, for example, look at just one corner with a highly discriminative piece pattern and neglect all other pieces. If skilled subjects select the cues properly, they are able to use their storage of task-specific knowledge, and this explains the superior skill of experts.

The experiments have demonstrated that the experts are significantly better than novices in recognizing chess positions. The experts have seen thousands of chess positions and this has created in their long-term memory a large store of chess-specific information. This database enables them to store a large set of positions to be recognized which a novice would not recognize. Improved recognition capacity is a consequence of chess training. It enables experts to use 'smaller' feature cues to distinguish the positions and hence to recognize the presented positions more effectively.

The results of recognition experiments thus support the traditional idea that experts are superior to novices because they are better able to recognize familiar solutions. They have just worked more and learned more task-specific patterns, which allows them to find effective hypotheses. Hence, we can fairly safely conclude that recognition can be an explanatory component in selective thinking.

Unfortunately, the recognition explanation leaves too many questions unanswered. It does not tell anything about the structure of recognized units. It does not tell which kind of elements the activated ideas entail nor how they are processed when they have been recognized. The recognition explanation does not provide us with an explanation for the selection among the possible recognizable alternatives. Certainly, experts can recognize more than one familiar idea in the positions. How do their minds select between preferable and non-preferable ideas? Moreover, recognition does not provide us with any knowledge about the representation of problems in memory. How are hypotheses stored? How much of the problem position is stored? In which memory system is the problem representation stored? What is relevant and what is irrelevant in a problem position?

Presumably, the most difficult conceptual problem with recognition is its 'conservatism'. We can recognize old solutions but cannot recognize new ones. Recognition means that we have already learned something and we simply retrieve this as an idea. Being limited in this way, recognition explains very little about creative problem solving. What recognition explains is the finding of standard ideas in standard positions. However, this is far from improving our understanding of really demanding problem solving and thinking.

MEMORY SYSTEMS

When ideas come to chess players' minds, their status in memory changes. The hypotheses which are actively studied are conscious and their contents are manipulated (cf. de Groot 1965). On the other hand, some hypotheses may temporarily be out of focus and also out of consciousness. This alternation of hypotheses between conscious and unconscious is probably associated with the structure of human memory and this is why the role of memory systems in selective thinking must be considered.

Traditionally human memory has been divided into subsystems (e.g. Atkinson and Shiffrin 1968, James 1890). Two of the subsystems, working memory and long-term memory, have been important in skills research (Atkinson and Shiffrin 1968, Baddeley 1990, Chase and Simon 1973a,b). Working memory is the main store for the active task-relevant information: that is, information manipulated during a particular task. Its capacity is limited and it has a modular structure (Baddeley 1986). Long-term memory is the store for all the knowledge we have in our brains and thus it also stores learned skills.

Besides attentional capacity limitations, working memory is a major 'bottleneck' in human information processing (Miller 1956, Shiffrin 1976, Waugh and Norman 1965). The number of separate items that can be kept actively in working memory is less than Miller's (1956) 7 ± 2; perhaps around 4 (Broadbent 1975, Simon 1974a, Watkins 1977). Such a small capacity must restrict all thought processes, and this is why the limits of working memory have been viewed as a major source of errors in thinking (Anderson and Jeffries 1985, Johnson-Laird 1983).

People easily overload their memories, forget something, lose their train of thought and, finally, end up with the wrong outcome. Almost any increase in the complexity of a task may increase the probability of errors. In decision-making experiments the increase of alternatives or attributes may impair the quality of decisions. Increasing the complexity often leads to the active pursuit of simplifications, which is a source of decision errors (Jungermann 1983, Montgomery and Svensson 1976, Payne 1982).

In deduction experiments, negations and other complexity-increasing factors are harmful, and in problem solving growing complexity causes an increase in error rates (Anderson 1987, Anderson and Jeffries 1985, Evans 1982, 1989). The number of analogous examples is fairly high, and one can safely assume that the capacity of working memory affects the quality of thought (Anderson and Jeffries 1985, Johnson-Laird 1983). Since the limited capacity of working memory is an important factor in the psychology of thinking, it cannot be ignored in discussing a thinking skill such as chess.

Several rather different models of working memory can be found in the literature (e.g. Anderson 1983, Atkinson and Shiffrin 1968, Baddeley 1986, Baddeley and Hitch 1974, Miller 1956). While the traditional models have postulated a single-capacity working memory, recent research has turned increasing attention to the modularity of human information processing (Atkinson and Shiffrin 1968, Baddeley 1986, Baddeley and Hitch 1974, Miller 1956, Simon 1974a, Waugh and Norman 1965).

Long-term memory has rarely been introduced in the discussion on capacity. It has normally been imagined to be a huge, somewhat passive store (Atkinson and Shiffrin 1968, Baddeley 1976, 1990).

Of course, forgetting and information structuring in long-term memory have long been studied, but this is not a capacity problem (e.g. Baddeley 1976, 1990, Bartlett 1932/1977). Nevertheless, long-term memory must be indirectly linked with processing capacity, since cognitive skills are stored in long-term memory. Training improves human performance and changes capacity. Consequently, the transcendence of capacity limits, a characteristic of experts, also requires discussion and research into experts' long-term memories.

It may be that new aspects of this problem can be found when experts' representations are thought out in detail. Accumulating evidence is showing that the two memory systems collaborate to maintain ongoing thinking (Chase and Ericsson 1982, Ericsson and Kintsch 1994). This means that long-term memory must have some responsibility for failures.

Other important questions can also be asked. For example, how are the tasks and subtasks allocated between the two main systems? This is an important question in all attempts to understand selective thinking, because the co-operation of the two memory systems is required in the controlling of conscious and unconscious processing. To make these issues clearer the research into chess players' memory must be reviewed. Fortunately, the research has been active and the main functions and properties of the memory systems are slowly becoming clearer.

RECALL OF CHESS POSITIONS

Recall is the basic paradigm for studying chess players' working memory, and the best-known working memory phenomenon is the expert superiority effect in recall. It was discovered by Djakov *et al.* (1926). These three Russian psychologists had noticed that skilled chess players remember chess positions better than less skilled ones. Of course, this was not a very dramatic finding, because the superiority of grandmaster memory was very evident in blindfold chess (Binet 1893/1966, Cleveland 1907). Nevertheless, these psychologists found arguments for the idea that chess players do not have a superior memory *per se*; their superiority is chess specific.

Djakov *et al.* (1926) showed one chess position for 1 minute to their subjects. The position was a chess problem. Chess problems are composed positions and close to random positions in their appearance, and, as the authors explicitly say, it would have been

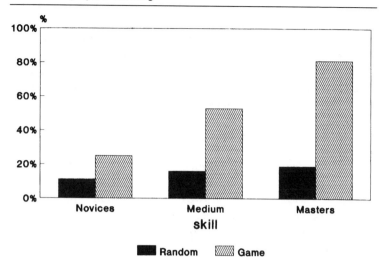

Figure 4.2 Recall of briefly presented random and game positions

better to have used a game position instead. It was fortunate, however, that they chose a sufficiently long presentation time, because with a shorter time they would probably not have found essential skill differences. Now they could report that after a 1-minute-long presentation their chess player subjects were three times better than non-chess players. In their other memory experiments, in which the stimuli consisted of dots on a chess board, numbers and geometric figures, no chess player superiority effect was found. As a consequence they concluded that chess players' superior memory is chess specific.

In the light of the earlier study, de Groot (1965, 1966) carried out an experiment showing that after a 2- to 15-second display, skilled chess players recalled real game positions better than less skilled players (see Figure 4.2). His experiment provided further evidence showing that the number of recalled pieces correlated with the level of skill. The more skilled a player the better was his or her recall. This result has since been confirmed several times (e.g. Chase and Simon 1973b, Saariluoma 1984, 1985).

The chess recall paradigm demonstrates not only the superiority of chess masters in recalling game positions but their weak performance in random positions, where all the pieces are scattered. For two decades many psychologists have mistakenly believed that de Groot (1965, 1966) was the first to experiment with random positions. However, Vicente and de Groot (1990) point out that in reality de Groot played no role in the experiments with random positions. The unpublished study that reported the experiments was actually carried out by Lemmens and Jongman. Nevertheless, the interaction between skill and the position type has been replicated and the results published several times since. Despite the confusion about the discoverer, the phenomenon itself is very reliable and easily replicable (Chase and Simon 1973b, Chi 1978, Frey and Adesman 1976, Saariluoma 1985).

Chess master superiority in recall can be found even with very short presentation times. Ellis (1973) in his thesis conducted an experiment in which by means of a tachistoscope he showed quadrants of a chessboard to his subjects for 150 milliseconds. He also varied the number of pieces in the stimulus and noticed that strong players were better than novices in recall, and that the number of pieces in the display increased the difference: the more pieces, the larger the difference.

The experts' superiority and the interaction between skill and the meaningful organization of the stimulus has proved to be very general. These effects have been replicated in different forms in many fields of expertise. Shneiderman (1976) found it in computer programming, Sloboda (1979) in music (see also McKeithen et al. 1981, Vicente 1988). Similarly, Go and bridge experts (Charness 1979, Engle and Bukstel 1978, Reitman 1976), electronics engineers (Egan and Schwartz 1979), trained map-readers (Gilhooly et al. 1988, Kinnear and Wood 1987), digit-remembering specialists (Chase and Ericsson 1982, Ericsson and Staszewski 1989), expert waiters (Ericsson and Polson 1988), good radiologists (Myles-Worsley et al. 1988), expert architects (Akin 1980), and even burglars (Logie et al. 1992) recall task-specific stimuli better than do novices.

The standard explanation for the interaction has been chunking (Chase and Simon 1973a, b). Masters' large stores of prelearned chunks produce high performance levels in recalling task-specific information (Charness 1988, 1989, 1992, Gilhooly and Green 1988, Saariluoma 1985, 1989). Skilled chess players have a large number of task-specific chunks in their long-term memories. When they are shown a chess position for a short time, they are able to encode the position in larger chunks (i.e. chess-specific patterns of pieces) than are novices, and therefore they are able to store more information about a position than are less experienced players (Chase and Simon

1973a, b). In the absence of familiar chunks expert chess players are unable to benefit from their vast storage of chess-specific knowledge and do not perform any better than novices in recalling random positions (Chase and Simon 1973b).

Working memory research has thus shown that expertise in chess recall tasks is based on cognitive elements that are similar to those found to be behind attentional superiority. Pieces, piece configurations and move sequences are associated in small clusters. Experts have a large store of these clusters in their memory and it seems that attentional modules and memory chunks are just two aspects of one and the same thing: learned chess-specific patterns.

THE ACTIVITY OF VISUAL WORKING MEMORY AND THE CENTRAL EXECUTIVE

The recall experiments demonstrate that working memory is involved in processing chess positions. The next question is, how are positions stored in working memory and what are the functions of this memory system in processing chess-specific information? If we understood better how tasks are allocated within working memory and between working memory and long-term memory we would undoubtedly have taken a big step towards understanding the function of memory systems in selective thinking.

Chase and Simon (1973b) originally assumed that working memory comprised a unitary store, as was generally assumed at the time. Later developments in memory research have, however, shown that working memory must be divided into modular subsystems. The results of experiments with visual and articulatory secondary tasks required the construction of a modular working memory (Baddeley 1983, 1986, Baddeley and Hitch 1974, Bradley *et al.* 1987, Robbins *et al.* in preparation). According to modular thinking, human working memory is divided into two main processing subsystems, which can be called visual working memory (or the visuo-spatial scratchpad) and the articulatory loop (Baddeley and Hitch 1974, Baddeley 1986). These two systems are independent but co-operate actively, and the allocation of resources between the two systems is controlled by the central executive. The modularity of the subsystems also means that they do not interfere with each other. If the articulatory loop is solely responsible for maintaining a process, this process cannot be interfered with by visual secondary tasks

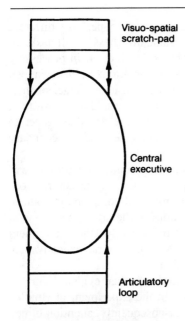

Visuo-spatial
scratch-pad

Central
executive

Articulatory
loop

Figure 4.3 The structure of the human working memory
Source: Baddeley (1986)

and vice versa. The modularity of working memory implies that the capacity-based selection may be partly modular.

Baddeley and Hitch's (1974) working memory model (see Figure 4.3) is also a capacity model (Baddeley 1986). The authors themselves rarely discuss capacity, and hence it may look as though the model has very little to do with capacity. Information format, i.e. visuo-spatial or articulatory, seems rather to be the fundamental conceptual postulate, i.e. an undefined, pretheoretical assumption. However, modular models of memory tacitly make capacity assumptions. Secondary task suppression is possible only if the processing capacity is limited and consequently the argument is very strongly grounded on within-subsystem capacity. Indeed, the load need not be intentionally conscious, because unattended information may affect the operations of the two slave systems (Logie 1986). The latter phenomenon is particularly interesting, because it eliminates possible attentional explanations.

The modular working memory theory raises an obvious but important question: what is the role of modularity in chess players' recall? Bradley *et al.* (1987) wanted to find an answer to this question. They instructed their subjects to perform different types of secondary tasks during a standard chess recall task. In this way they could selectively suppress the three main processing systems. In the visuo-spatial suppression conditions, subjects tapped in a circle on the computer keyboard with the index finger of their left hand. In the articulatory conditions they repeated the word 'the', and in central executive conditions they were asked to generate numbers randomly. In the control conditions they had no secondary task.

Only in the visuo-spatial and central executive conditions was subjects' performance substantially lower than in the control conditions. Articulatory interference was minimal compared to control. The results suggest that subjects do not use the articulatory loop at all in encoding chess positions. Consequently, the experiment suggests that visuo-spatial memory and the central executive are occupied in the recall of chess positions.

Saariluoma (1991a, 1992a) has found further evidence for the importance of visuo-spatial memory. In the experiment of Bradley *et al.* (1987) only recall was studied. Subsequently, attention turned to information intake and the calculation of variations. Subjects'

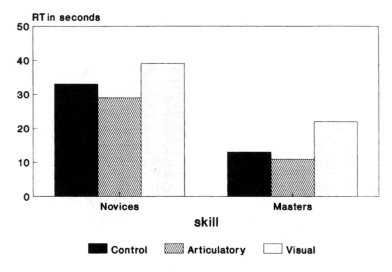

Figure 4.4 Visuo-spatial and articulatory secondary task effects on chess players' information intake. Subjects at master and novice level were asked whether a one-move mate was possible under three secondary task conditions

performance in perceptual classification tasks were compared under imaging and articulatory suppression. Whereas articulatory tasks did not have a significant effect on subjects' information intake, a secondary imaging task (i.e. Brooks's (1968) letter task) did have a strong inhibiting effect (Saariluoma 1992a) (see Figure 4.4). In a thinking-aloud method with suppression tasks, a large impairment was found in the number of generated moves in imaging suppression conditions, but no corresponding articulatory impairment could be measured (Saariluoma 1991a).

Like Bradley *et al.* (1987) in memory recall tasks, Holding (1989) interfered with the move generation procedure using a backwards counting task. Holding (1989) is apt to interpret impairment in calculations as articulatory interference, but it may be that it is due rather to central executive interference, because backwards counting loads the central executive quite strongly. The visuo-spatial scratch-pad and central executive are essential components in chess players' information processing, while in the light of current evidence the articulatory loop seems relatively unimportant.

The modular working memory provides a more precise explanation for chess players' memory performance than does the classic short-term memory model. It is especially important to notice that the modular working memory explains not only the existence of strong visuo-spatial interference, but also the almost total absence of articulatory suppression effects.

VISUAL IMAGERY

The experiments described in the previous section showed that chess players' memory used visual working memory very actively, but relied very little on phonological or articulatory-based memory. Because visual working memory is normally taken as practically equivalent to visual imagery, the results convincingly demonstrate the active role of visual imagery in chess players' thinking (Baddeley 1986, 1990). In such a visually oriented task environment as chess, visual imagery obviously becomes an important medium for thought and it must be considered thoroughly.

Visual imagery and imagination have always been important notions in chess players' lay psychology (Abrahams 1951, Blumenfeld 1948, Krogius 1976). Chess players are not allowed to touch the pieces when they think, and must therefore carry out all the manipulations in their visual imagery. This practical experience of chess players makes the problems of mental imagery important in lay psychological theories. Evidence for the lay psychology view can, in addition to working memory experiments, be found from experiments that directly focus on mental imagery in chess.

Church and Church (1977) reported an experiment in which, on an empty board, they varied the distance of a checking piece from the king. They noticed that the processing times with pieces that move diagonally (i.e. the queen or the bishop) were strongly correlated with distance, whereas when queen or rook were moved horizontally processing times were much less influenced by distance.

A very similar experiment to that reported by Church and Church (1977) was conducted by Milojkovic (1982). Using a tachistoscope he presented his subjects with chess positions containing three pieces for a period of 3 seconds. Immediately after that he showed a card whose colour indicated the move to be imagined. When Milojkovic varied the distance between the pieces, the reaction times of novice subjects increased with the increased distance, but no effect was apparent with masters. Possibly the masters had strong automatized attentional modules for moves, or possibly they were able to encode both threats during the initial 3-second period, and thus they did not need to carry out any mental transformations when the instruction card appeared. However, Saariluoma's (1984) results on single threat detection support the former explanation.

The problem of imagery control was raised by Bachmann and Oit (1992). They used Attneave and Curlee's (1982) moving spot task. Subjects were instructed to move a spot or a chess piece within an imaginary grid following given instructions. They found that skilled chess players were better than non-skilled players in moving a chess piece in their imagery, though no essential differences could be found in moving a spot. The authors argued that the representation is neither purely propositional nor purely pictorial in chess imagery.

Visual imagery in chess is not just imagery. It also has contents, and empirical knowledge about the active involvement of conceptual processes in imaging supports the relevance of content-specific processes. On the other hand the properties of this format are important *per se*. The analogue properties of images of objects, for example, affect processing speed. It seems also to be the case that imagery formation depends on skill. The more skilled a player the easier it is for that player to construct a chess-specific image. The blindfold chess experiments that are reviewed below provide further support for the idea that chess players' images depend essentially on chess-specific patterns of pieces.

THE FUNCTIONS OF WORKING MEMORY

What is the role of working memory in encoding and storing chess positions? The research inspired by the modular working memory model of Baddeley and Hitch (1974) has introduced an interesting response to this question. Visuo-spatial working memory is normally used for mental transformations and these operations are needed when calculating variations (Bundesen and Larsen 1975, Chase and Simon 1973a,b, Cooper and Shepard 1973, Saariluoma 1991a, Shepard and Metzler 1971). This is why visuo-spatial suppression has a marked influence on the generation in think-aloud protocols (Saariluoma 1991a). Mental manipulation of positions is therefore the first function of visual working memory in chess.

One does not, however, need mental transformation in recall experiments. In fact, mental transformation may have a negative effect, because it may result in a large number of translation errors in recall experiments (Chase and Simon 1973a, b). A translation

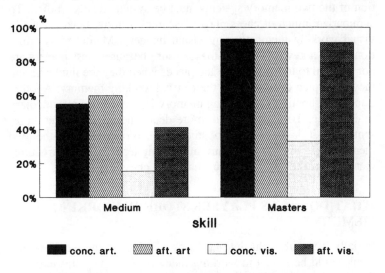

Figure 4.5 Visual interference in auditory presentation. Subjects' recall of chess positions was impaired by giving them a concurrent, secondary visuo-spatial task; thought presentation was auditory

error appears when a correct piece is recalled as being one or two squares from its actual location. Since the visual suppression effect is so clear in the experiments of Bradley *et al.* (1987), visual working memory must serve some function other than mental transformation. That function must be encoding and elaboration of information for long-term memory storage.

Saariluoma (1989) asked subjects to recall chess positions that were presented auditorily in the form of named pieces together with the board co-ordinates of their squares (e.g. white bishop h2). At the same time subjects carried out either a visuo-spatial or an articulatory secondary task. In concurrent conditions suppression took place during the whole presentation time. In subsequent conditions subjects first had an opportunity to encode the positions, and only after that did they carry out the secondary task. Substantial interference was found only in concurrent visual suppression conditions. This result strongly suggests that visual working memory is important in encoding but is no longer significant when the position has been encoded and moved into long-term memory. It means that visual working memory is used for temporary storage during elaboration but long-term memory is actively used to support the storage operations in working memory. Consequently, the co-operation of the two memory systems must be systematically studied. To summarize: much of chess players' search for moves takes place in visual working memory using visual imagery. Mental transformations have a key role, which makes sense because chess players are not allowed to touch or move the pieces when they are thinking, and they must plan everything in their visual working memory. Another important function for working memory is to act as an intermediary in encoding. To understand in more detail the nature of the representation, it is necessary to study the co-operation of the two memory systems and the nature of the long-term memory structures that support the superior performance of chess masters.

WHAT DO CHESS PLAYERS STORE IN WORKING MEMORY?

Initially it was thought that the chess positions in the recall experiment would be stored in working memory. However, this explanation has been regarded as doubtful for some time, and evidence against the possible involvement of storage in working memory has gradually increased (Chase and Simon 1973a,b). The problem was

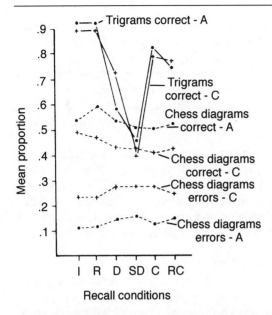

Figure 4.6 The effects of backward counting on the recall of chess position and trigrams. With trigrams, substantial impairment was noticed but with chess positions there was practically no impairment as a consequence of the Brown–Peterson task
Source: Charness (1976)

first raised by Alan Allport (1975) in his critical commentary on Chase and Simon's (1973b) publication. Allport argued that chess recall experiments cannot be directly compared with classic working memory experiments such as list learning. He did not, however, conduct any experiments to confirm his ideas.

The first experimental work on the topic was published by Charness (1976) on the basis of his earlier thesis (Charness 1974). He found the surprising result that the recall of chess positions cannot be interfered with using the Brown–Peterson paradigm; that is, by asking subjects to count backwards for 30 seconds between presentation and recall (Figure 4.6). In contrast, this secondary task interferes strongly with the recall of nonsense syllables (Brown 1958, Peterson and Peterson 1959).

Frey and Adesman (1976) set up a similar problem to Charness (1976), presenting to their subjects either one or two successive positions. Their argument was that if one position filled working memory, then subjects could not recall more than one position when presented with two successive positions. If subjects could store more chunks from two positions than they could from a single position, this would contradict the working memory hypothesis. Since subjects could recall around twelve pieces from single positions and nineteen from two successive positions, the results falsified the hypothesis that chess positions were stored in the limited-capacity working memory.

Holding (1985) made a further important observation. He pointed out that the number of chunks in Chase and Simon's (1973b) experiments was larger than one would expect. Thirteen chunks registered on the basis of between-piece latencies was more than the assumed limited capacity of working memory. This meant that the basic empirical evidence contradicted the working memory storage hypothesis.

The discussion that has taken place in recent years generally opposes the working memory storage hypothesis. If chess players stored chess positions in their working memories, they should be filled with the chunks needed in storing one position but then there would no longer be any extra space left for another position. Since the number of pieces chess players recall from two positions is almost double the number of pieces recalled from one position, the working memory storage hypothesis cannot be correct. Consequently, researchers have generally abandoned the idea of working memory storage and suggested that chess positions are stored in long-term memory (Charness 1976, Frey and Adesman 1976, Lane and Robertson 1979, Simon 1976).

The experiments in this section confirm that chess players use their long-term memory very actively to store chess-specific information. This suggests that the co-operation of the two memory systems is vital in thinking, and, consequently, the co-operation of memory systems must be analysed in detail. A suitable task for exploring this kind of issue is provided by blindfold chess.

BLINDFOLD CHESS

In blindfold chess, players do not see the board or the pieces and the opponent's moves are given by using the names of the pieces and their board co-ordinates (e.g. bishop from c4 to f7). Consequently, blindfold players must rely totally on their visual memory and mental imagery when playing. Naturally, their opponents may see the board and the pieces, though this is not essential from our point of view.

The most impressive form of this task is simultaneous blindfold chess. Here a blindfold player plays against several relatively strong opponents at the same time. Since the number of games can be as high as twenty to fifty, the memory load is enormous (see Holding 1985 for the world records). The play is so taxing that blindfold exhibitions were forbidden by law in the former Soviet Union (see Wason's comment 1 in Binet 1893/1966, p. 131). There is anecdotal evidence that somebody actually died while attempting to beat the world record.

The exceptionally high memory load is the very reason why psychologists have been interested in blindfold chess for so long. Blindfold chess provides evidence of the extreme limits of human memory. When people play tens of chess games simultaneously without any external support, the memory load greatly exceeds the normal limits of working memory and thus the memory load is an argument for the relevance of the task as a testing ground for the co-operation of the two memory systems.

Binet (1893/1966) made a thorough study of the issue. His work contains many stimulating ideas, but being a non-chess player he was, as de Groot (1965) has pointed out, duped by the masters he interviewed. He believed, for example, that chess masters can calculate hundreds of moves before making one. Nevertheless, Binet's (1893/1966) work offers a very interesting inside view of blindfold chess by letting chess masters report their own experiences of blindfold play.

In the study, the chess masters reported that they could not remember games unless they understood them, which suggests that the encoding was at a deep semantic level (Craik and Lockhart 1972, Goldin 1978a) Similar remarks were made by experienced subjects in a study carried out almost a hundred years later (Saariluoma 1991b). The masters interviewed by Binet (1893/ 1966) also emphasized the importance of concentration and the abstractness of the representation. Both seem to be valid properties of blindfold chess players' experience even today.

Cleveland (1907) followed Binet in his study of blindfold chess, and made a number of significant observations. Pillsbury, a well-known grandmaster, grouped games using the same opening in each game of a group, a strategy adopted to make chunking easier. Pillsbury also tried to keep in mind some distinctive features of the games in order to recall them more easily. The representation, according to Cleveland (1907), is partial and concentrated on the area of the board where the most interesting conflicts take place. Finally, he argued that a player could learn to play chess without ever having seen a chessboard, with the task chosen to be as difficult as possible. Reuben Fine (1965), a former world-class chess player and well-known psychoanalyst, published a very interesting introspective and retrospective paper on his own blindfold chess experiences. The greatest problems in playing blindfold chess were, in Fine's opinion, precise visualization of the board and the differentiation of the games from each other. As a consequence, he felt eased if someone made an uncommon move in order to try to trick him and make him forget the game, because the ability to discriminate the position was so greatly enhanced. He also emphasized the importance of meaningful associations, and spatial and temporal Gestalts, i.e. chunks.

Ericsson and Staszewski (1989) report a study made by Ericsson and Oliver some years earlier. They studied a chess player who was rated a little lower than the master level. He was studied using several experimental tasks related to skilled memory theory. The player was asked, among other things, to report on a piece on a nominated square (e.g. a4) to count the pieces in a submatrix of four squares (a1, a2, b1, b2), both when the row or column was visible and when it was imagined. In recalling single pieces their chess player was minimally faster in perceptual than in imagery conditions, but in the two other subtasks he was two to three seconds faster in perceptual than imagery conditions. The player was thus able to access information on any square of a chessboard within seconds and he could very freely access information from his mental imagery.

Saariluoma (1991b) wanted to conduct experiments on blindfold chess directly aimed at analysing skill differences. In these experiments a systematic skill effect, visual spatial secondary task impairment and large memory load effects were shown. In all seven experiments, which were conducted on different aspects of the blindfold game, experts surpassed novices. It was also shown that visuo-spatial secondary tasks impaired performance, while articulatory tasks had no substantial effect. This implies that visual working memory is actively used in blindfold chess. Finally, an experiment was conducted in which subjects were read out ten simultaneous blindfold games in conditions resembling those of

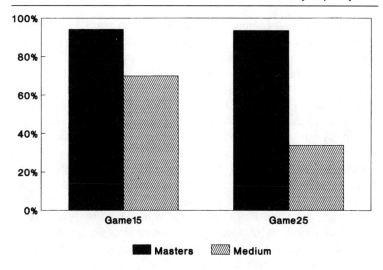

Figure 4.7 Blindfold chess. The percentage of correctly recalled piece locations after 15 and 25 moves in groups of master-strength and medium-strength groups of players

actual blindfold exhibitions. The experiment showed that really strong chess players can follow all games without errors, though a depth of six moves is too much for novices (see Figure 4.7).

Blindfold chess shows that imagery in chess is based on pre-learned chess-specific patterns. Experts who have this knowledge are able to carry out these very demanding memory recall tasks, but are not able to succeed in these tasks at all. The imagery in chess is chess-specific and arises as a consequence of training.

Memory load differences are very large: whereas the locations of a few pieces are too much for novices, experts are able to store thousands of piece locations. It can be argued that these locations are meaningful, but they are not meaningful *per se*. It is the skill of masters that gives the pieces and their locations meaning.

Blindfold chess implies a strong connection between human conceptual systems and mental imagery. In order to play rational blindfold chess the pieces must be moved precisely to particular squares. However, there is no imagery-level explanation as to why some of the squares would be more important than others (Saari-luoma 1991b). Consequently, the conceptual system must interact with imagery to maintain blindfold play (Bachmann and Oit 1992).

Finally, the blindfold experiments illustrate the co-operation of the two memory systems. It is not possible to store several chess games simultaneously in the limited-capacity working memory. This means that the subjects build into their long-term memories retrieval structures and store the games and relevant positions into these structures (Chase and Ericsson 1973a, b, Ericsson and Staszewski 1989, Ericsson and Kintsch 1994). They use the retrieval structures selectively and access the presently relevant parts. The manipulations and encoding take place in working memory.

When information is in working memory, it is in a very unstable state and it can be interfered with by appropriate secondary tasks. Loss of information and forgetting is the consequence of that interference. Of course, if the long-term memory load becomes very high, there are limits on how much can be retrieved. However, this long-term memory 'overloading' depends on skill. The more skilled a player the more complex the representations that he or she is able to construct and remember.

CO-OPERATION BETWEEN THE TWO MEMORY SYSTEMS

Information needed in working memory must be accessed from the long-term memory. Information must also be transferred to long-term memory and this is why the co-operation of the two memory systems is an important problem in chess psychology. We are still quite unfamiliar with how chess players' memory systems have organized this co-operation and several problems require an explanation. In the next few pages I shall try to provide some answers.

The first problem is encoding and information transfer to long-term memory. The skilled memory theory predicts that the most familiar patterns are swiftly stored in long-term memory (Chase and Ericsson 1981, 1982, Ericsson and Staszewski 1989). However, the less familiar ones are stored slowly. Similar suggestions have also been made by Chase and Simon (1973a, b) and Charness (1976).

If we look at the number of encoded pieces as a function of the presentation time, the skilled memory theory would predict a negatively accelerating function, because the familiar patterns are coded first swiftly and the rest of the representation must be encoded slowly. Saariluoma (1984) found precisely this kind of learning curve for chess players' recall (see Figure 4.8).

The next problem concerns the accessing of chunks in long-term memory. When a chess player is presented with a chess position he

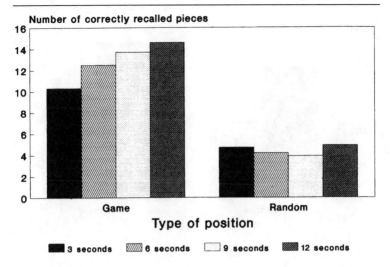

Figure 4.8 Presentation time and recall. Recall of game and random positions after 3, 6, 9 and 12 seconds

or she must encode it using the storage of chess-specific patterns. A major question is the kind of information access processes that are required. The key empirical issue is the recall of random positions, because experts' failures with these positions provide important information about the information retrieval and access mechanisms.

A very straightforward interpretation of the skilled memory theory, for example, would suggest that the reason why skilled chess players fail when attempting to recall random positions is that they contain no chunks. Because experts can benefit from their chunks only when there are chunks in a game position, it is logical to argue that the failure with random positions is caused by the absence of chunks. Chess players do not play random chess, and this is why their long-term knowledge base simply does not contain information about random piece patterns. They do not have any retrieval structures for recalling random information. However, this direct chunking interpretation is too simple, and more complex mechanisms must be assumed. Hunt and Love (1972) studied a mnemonist. In one of their subtasks they presented game positions and random positions to their subject, who was a strong chess player. They noticed that their subject could learn game positions faster than random positions, but he could also learn random positions relatively swiftly, i.e. in less than a minute. The results

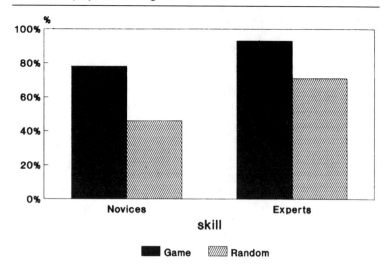

Figure 4.9 Lories's (1987) results on long presentation times. Experts and novices were presented with game and random positions for 1 minute. Experts are better at recalling random positions as well as game positions

suggest that chess experts might be able to learn random positions more quickly than has been assumed earlier. Since there were no control experiments with novices, the experiment did not lead to a breakthrough in chess psychology. None the less, fifteen years later the encoding of random positions by experts did attract the attention of psychologists interested in chess.

Lories (1987) presented game and random positions for one minute to his subjects. Surprisingly, he found no interaction between game and random positions (see Figure 4.9). Experts were better, as one might expect, in recalling game positions, but they were also superior to the novices in recalling random positions.

If we think of the standard explanation for the failure of experts in recalling random positions, Lories (1987) did uncover a paradox. It was earlier claimed that it is the absence of chunks in random positions which explains why experts fail. However, if the absence of chunks were the reason, the experts should have failed whatever presentation times were used.

Saariluoma (1989) presented subjects with chess positions auditorily, confirming Lories's (1987) findings. When subjects were presented with only one random position, skilled subjects clearly

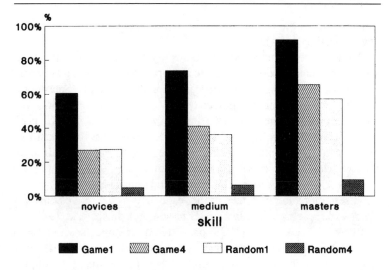

Figure 4.10 Recall of auditorily presented game and random positions by masters, medium-strength players and novices

recalled more than less skilled subjects (see Figure 4.10). This was not particularly surprising, because in auditory presentation the reading time of twenty to twenty-five pieces is inevitably close to one minute. However, when the number of random positions to be recalled at one time was raised from one to four, the experts lost control of the material to be memorized. Since they did not have great difficulty in recalling a series of four-game positions, the interaction between skill and the type of positions was again confirmed. Though experts did not encounter many difficulties in remembering four real game positions, they could not retain four random positions because of very strong interference between the positions. The experts met with great difficulty deciding as to the positions of the chunks that they could remember and very soon their representation totally collapsed.

Results showed that the complete absence of chunks in random positions is not the reason for their poor recall in short presentation times, and consequently direct chunking provides an inadequate account. It is the available time and not the absence of chunks which is decisive. If this piece of knowledge is put together with the knowledge that the absolute locations of the chunks are relevant, it suggests that locations might be an important retrieval cue. Extra time is required if a perfect match does not exist. This would suggest that in the case of chess the retrieval structure contains low-level location knowledge.

Another problematic aspect of the results of long auditory presentation recall experiments is the disappearance of skill differences in random positions with increasing memory load (Saariluoma 1989). Though skilled subjects were superior in recalling one random position they lost their grasp with four successive positions. The subjects were again able to learn the four positions when they had unlimited learning time, but the results still show that overload may cause a total loss of control over the random positions. The integration, elaboration and construction of long-term representations in chess takes time, especially if the moves have not been well practised in advance (Ericsson and Staszewski 1989).

Recently Cooke *et al.* (1993) presented their subjects with a series of one, three, five, seven and nine successive positions. Each position was shown for 8 seconds. They found that the subjects recalled on average fewer pieces per position when the number of presented positions increased. Gobet and Simon (1994a) have found a similar phenomenon, but their effects are even stronger than the ones of Cooke *et al.* (1993), because they used shorter presentations. The results suggest that subjects' ability to swiftly encode positions into the long-term memory retrieval structures is limited. The differences in procedures seem to imply that encoding time is one essential explanatory factor.

The co-ordination and control of information transmission between the two memory systems thus bring to the fore a new aspect of memory capacity, an aspect that very much depends on skill. This is information encoding and elaboration using pre-learned memory structures. Unless subjects have had sufficient time to build the retrieval structures, the representation collapses.

LONG-TERM KNOWLEDGE BASE IN CHESS

Long-term memory retrieval structures are crucial in explaining chess players' skill differences and other recall-related memory phenomena. However, nothing has been said so far about what these retrieval structures are like. What kind of information and how that information is organized in long-term memory are open problems.

Chase and Simon (1973a,b) were the first to analyse representational issues, and their work provided the first important information

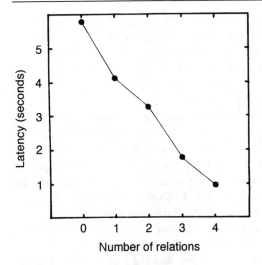

Figure 4.11 Chess-specific relations and recall. The researchers related the average recall latency between two chess pieces and the number of chess-specific relations, i.e. threat, defence, colour, kind and adjacency, between them
Source: Chase and Simon (1973b)

about chess players' long-term knowledge base. They modified the memory recall task and presented subjects with several 5-second displays until the subjects achieved almost total recall of the presented positions. The maximum number of presentations was six. Chase and Simon (1973b) observed that subjects' recall was organized into clusters of a few pieces, which, following Miller (1956), they referred to as chunks. The pieces in the chunks seemed to have higher-level interpiece relations such as attack (either one of the two successively recalled pieces attacked the other), defence (either of the pieces defended the other), proximity (each piece occupies one of the eight squares adjacent to the others), common colour (both pieces have the same colour) and kind (both pieces are of the same type, for example pawns).

The chess-specific relations, as these relations were referred to, were important because the probability of subsequent recall correlated with the number of chess-specific relations between the pieces (Figure 4.11). The Chase and Simon (1973a,b) experiments involved just four subjects, so their reliability may be questionable. However, very recently, Gold and Opwis (1992) replicated their experiment and showed that Chase and Simon's empirical results were reliable. Gobet and Simon (1994b) have also analysed chess masters' chunking. As a consequence of improved response measurement, they have found substantially larger chunks than before in master players' recall. Nevertheless, their overall results are in harmony with the previous findings.

The connection between the number of chess-specific relations and recall latencies is only correlational. In chess it is logical that attack, defence, proximity, colour and kind are important. Pawn chains and systems of attack and defence form an essential part of chess knowledge. Therefore, chunks or chess-specific patterns are also functional units in chess, and a natural representational format for chess-specific knowledge in the long-term memory.

This information can be very effectively described with network structures such as EPAM and its derivatives (Simon and Barenfeld 1969, Simon and Chase 1973, Simon and Gilmartin 1973). The key idea in these models is that a chunk can be described as object–relation–object triplet. In it chess-specific relations are represented by arcs and the nodes can be assumed to contain information about pieces. While Chase and Simon's (1973a,b) experiments provided solid support for the importance of chess-specific relations in long-term storage, they provide few, if any, data about node information, i.e. what is coded about the pieces.

Three types of chess-relevant information can be coded about a piece: form, colour and location. Since it is evident that form and colour must be coded to define the piece concerned, the key problem is the status of location coding. Do we represent the locations of the chunked pieces, or do we just represent the forms of chunks in long-term memory? This question was raised by Holding (1985) when he argued against the importance of chess-specific patterns in explaining chess skill. Holding argued that Chase and Simon's (1973a,b) estimates of the number of stored chunks in long-term memory (Simon and Gilmartin 1973) were far too large. Simon and Chase (1973) tacitly assumed that chess players stored the absolute locations of the pieces in their long-term memories and Simon and Gilmartin (1973) posited this explicitly (see also Chase and Simon 1973a,b). Holding (1985) criticized this idea by pointing out that chess players can recognize any chess-specific pattern even if it is moved one or two squares. Whereas the supporters of absolute location coding assumed that patterns located in two different places on the chessboard are different even when they have the same form (e.g. white pawns on a2, b2 and on d4, e4), Holding (1985) argued for relative location coding.

Saariluoma (1984, 1994) conducted experiments to find empirical evidence and showed that the location of a chunk had an effect on its recallability even when its form had not changed (Figure 4.12). If chunks in a presented position are in their original locations on the board, they are easier to encode and recall than if they are transposed from their original location. This suggests that information on spatial location is an essential part of the knowledge stored in chunks. The importance of chess-specific relations and location information in the recall of chess positions suggests that chunks have a complex structure in which very different types of information are encoded and relevant.

Freyhof et al. (1992) asked subjects to partition chess positions into meaningful units. After the first partition subjects were asked to partition basic-level chunks into subgroups and classify them into supergroups. Interestingly, masters created larger piece clusters at all levels than medium players. Also, in typical positions the piece groups were larger than in atypical positions. Therefore, the authors

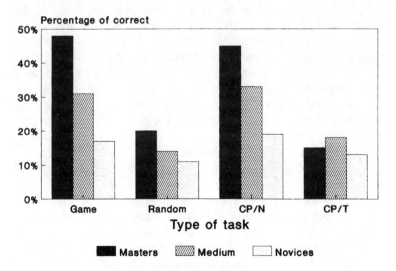

Figure 4.12 Recall of correctly located and dislocated areas. Game = game positions, Random = random positions, CP/N = composed positions with normally located quadrants, CP/T = composed positions with transposed quadrants

argued that the partitioning process provides evidence about the hierarchical structure of chess knowledge.

Gold and Opwis (1992) also studied the chunk sizes and noticed that, in general, experts are able to construct larger chunks than novices. They found, however, that Chase and Simon's (1973b) 2-second criterion for a border between chunks was problematic, though it works mostly well (cf. Gobet and Simon 1994b). The latter had argued that interpiece intervals that were longer than 2 seconds meant that two successive pieces belonged to different chunks, while the shorter interpiece intervals signified that they belonged to the same chunk. As Gold and Opwis (1992) pointed out, the 2-second criterion is somewhat arbitrary and longer criterion times lead to larger chunks, whereas shorter criterion times lead to a larger number of chunks with fewer pieces. Consequently, Gold and Opwis adopted a hierarchical cluster analysis, and reported substantial differences in clusters between experts and novices. They also reported substantial differences between real and random positions in the chunks. In the former position types, king's side, queen's side and centre formed independent units, while in the latter position types the chunks were substantially more random.

All studies referred to so far have converged on recall or the partitioning of positions. The recall of a position is not necessarily the same thing as the recall of a game. Fine (1965) argues that chess players' ability to remember blindfold games (that is, games which are played without seeing the board or pieces) depends on spatial and temporal 'Gestalts'. The location patterns are static spatial Gestalts, and familiar move sequences represent dynamic and temporal Gestalts. Since chunking was not as universally accepted a psychological term in 1965 as it is today, Fine referred instead to two categories: spatial and temporal Gestalts.

Fine seemed to suggest that chess games and different types of 'subgames', such as the themes of combinations, familiar man-oeuvres and other items of temporal chess-specific knowledge, are stored using the same basic memory mechanisms that are used in storing spatial chess specific patterns. The only difference is the content of the material to be stored. This means that chunks contain in addition to a piece pattern also a short sequence of moves.

Chase and Simon (1973b) conducted experiments to support this view. They asked chess players of different strengths to learn chess games and found that skilled chess players clearly needed a shorter time to learn a chess game than less skilled players. They also showed that subjects really do use spatio-temporal chunks in building their representation of games.

In the blindfold chess experiments discussed above, Saariluoma (1991a) found more evidence for the chunking of temporal patterns. Subjects were blindfolded and heard descriptions of three different types of games: a real game, a random game with legal moves and a random game with illegal moves. The normal game was the easiest to follow, but the random game with legal moves was not much more difficult for the experts. The random game with illegal moves was almost impossible for experts. The reason was that subjects could not use their temporal move patterns in random games with illegal moves. In the random game with legal moves, the play developed far more slowly and resulted in unfamiliar positions. However, because legal moves were involved the experts were able to take advantage of their greater degree of chess-specific knowledge.

Experiments with game recall and blindfold chess thus support the generalizability of chunking models, such as the skilled memory theory (Ericsson and Staszewski 1989). The basic database in chess players' long-term memory consists of a set of spatio-temporal piece and move patterns.

However, in addition to piece locations, chess-specific relations and move sequences, higher-level information is also coded in chess players' long-term memory. This was demonstrated by Pfau and Murphy (1988). They found that verbal knowledge must also be an essential part of the long-term memory knowledge base in chess. They constructed a set of chess-specific tasks or 'tests' concerning recall of verbal knowledge, tactical skill and positional judgement and correlated these measures with skill. They found, surprisingly, that tactical knowledge, positional knowledge and verbal knowledge were clearly better predictors of chess skill than memory recall. The results suggest that spatio-temporal patterns, which are important in tactical chess, are vital for high-level chess, but they also suggest that positional and verbal knowledge are very important predictors. Both of the latter two tests emphasize the importance of verbal knowledge, because positional evaluation is often based on verbally expressible rules (see also Cooke et al. 1993).

Experimental work has so far concentrated on chess-specific patterns that represent relatively low-level information of mostly a tacit and analogous nature. There is very little doubt that this storage of spatio-temporal patterns is an important part of chess players' long-term memory. The main content of these patterns is chess-specific relations, pieces and their locations. In addition, static patterns are often associated with a dynamic move series.

Recent research suggests, however, that chess-specific patterns are not the only type of knowledge in chess players' memory. Verbal knowledge about chess, its history and information about the strategic rules needed in positional judgement are also important and cannot be neglected in chess psychology. The focus can now be moved from the structural to the functional aspects of chess memory.

MEMORY CAPACITY AND CHESS SKILL

Memory is essential in chess. Skilled chess players have to remember thousands of opening variations, endgame and middle game position types and combinations. Their trained 'vocabulary' for chess-specific materials is around 50,000 to 100,000 patterns (Chase and Simon 1973b, Simon and Gilmartin 1973). In nearly all cases the time needed to learn all this is at least ten years (Chase and Simon 1973b). In the time required to achieve a high level of expertise, chess is in no way different from any other field of expertise (Hayes 1981, 1985).

This training helps chess players to develop a very efficient task-specific memory, though their basic memory capacity remains unchanged. They sometimes call this task-specific memory ability 'chess memory', which is simply a memory for task-specific materials, i.e. a skilled memory (Ericsson and Kintsch 1994). The experiments have constantly shown that the lay concept of chess memory is very real. Experts are superior to novices in recalling and recognizing chess-specific materials from single positions to games and series of simultaneous blindfold games (e.g. Charness 1976, Chase and Simon 1973a, b, de Groot 1965, Saariluoma 1984). However, a phenomenal chess memory is not a sign of a phenomenal memory and several capacity limitations must be kept in mind when discussing chess players' memory.

Chess players' working memory has a modular structure and also contains module-specific capacity limitations. Visual and central executive secondary tasks cause significant impairment in recall, stimulus processing, and the calculation of variations (Bradley *et al.* 1987, Holding 1989, Saariluoma 1991a, 1992a).

Information transmission and elaboration is very strongly affected by skill. Pre-learned information structures can be encoded very quickly into long-term memory, while less familiar and unfamiliar structures require time-consuming operations (Charness 1976, Chase and Ericsson 1981, 1982, Chase and Simon 1973b, Ericsson and Staszewski 1989). Of course, when the length of encoding time increases, the probability of interference also grows, and therefore the most familiar chunks are very probably recalled the best.

Chess memory thus contains different types of capacity limitations. First, subsystems or modules have limits on their capacity to carry out concurrent tasks. Second, long-term memory encoding takes time. Third, constructing retrieval structures in long-term memory is limited by skill level and naturally cannot be infinite. There is at the moment no reason to believe that skill would greatly affect the capacity of the working memory subsystems to carry out unrelated tasks. The speed of encoding and the size of relatively swiftly constructed retrieval systems are, on the contrary, clearly dependent on skill. The more skilled the individual, the more effectively he or she can use the pre-learned knowledge structures to transmit information into long-term memory.

CAPACITY AND CALCULATION

The most evident consequence of limited working memory capacity can be found in the calculation of variations. Chess players do not generate long move sequences, because they are not able to do so. Their working memory limits the calculation and thus limits also the extent of the representations.

The research into the number of generated moves has provided somewhat contradictory results. One of de Groot's (1965) main findings was the modest size of the experts' search. Subjects generated only a fraction of all possible moves. Even more surprising was the small size of the skill-related individual differences in the size of the search spaces. Skilled chess players did not search through essentially larger spaces than did less skilled players. The later research contrasts with de Groot's (1965) findings. Charness (1981a) has found material to support the superior size of skilled chess players' subjective search spaces. In his experiments thirty-two subjects were shown four chess positions and noticed that the maximum depth increased by nearly 1.5 plies per standard deviation of skill. (One ply is equal to one move either by White or by Black.)

Finally, Saariluoma (1990b) observed that his international-level players did not have as broad a search as national masters and yet they reached a higher percentage of correct solutions. However, Saariluoma (1992b) also showed that skilled and less skilled chess players respectively in endgame positions calculate a very different number of moves.

These results suggest that skilled chess players are sometimes able to achieve the goal with less search, but sometimes it is necessary for them to build larger subjective search spaces. The contradiction between the results of Saariluoma (1990b), Charness (1981a) and de Groot (1965) can perhaps best be explained by the task difficulty. Good chess players are able to count longer variations and search more continuations if they feel it is necessary, but if the tasks happen to be easy for them they do not need to search so widely or deeply. They simply do not need to do unnecessary work and their search is optimal. Some evidence for this idea was found in an unpublished analysis of four hundred chess games which was made by the grandmaster Yrjö Rantanen. In these analyses it was noticed that skilled chess players' combinations were some two moves longer than non-skilled chess players' combinations.

Experts are able to construct longer memory representations, when required. In a complicated battle this ability means that experts can foresee the consequences of moves a little further ahead than can novices and this ability may be decisive for the whole course of the game. In this way experts' ability to circumvent their limited memory capacity and construct wider representations may often be very decisive for the outcome of the game. This phenomenon demonstrates that the limited working memory capacity is an essential factor in chess players' information processing, although it does not alone provide a sufficient explanation. A move or two extra in the calculation does not mean much on its own when we consider that the number of possible move combinations rises easily to millions.

MEMORY AND THINKING

The properties of human memory provide information that is relevant in the interpretation of several aspects of selective thinking. The phenomena associated with recognition explain how learned information can be used during thinking. The familiar aspects of situation are recognized and the corresponding ideas are activated.

When an idea is activated and it is actively processed this takes place in working memory. The role of visual working memory is particularly important. The subjects use visual working memory or imagery to simulate the consequences of moves. This is logical because the reviewed empirical research strongly suggests that the main function of working memory is the active manipulation of information needed in searching for a move. This is also in agreement with the general idea that the main function of visual imagery in thinking is information manipulation (Denis 1991).

The capacity of working memory is limited. Infinitely large move networks cannot be actively manipulated in them, and if the capacity is surpassed errors will follow. Several arguments for the working memory capacity based error theory can be suggested. The size of the move networks increases with increasing skill. If the players are forced to construct large working memory representations, the experts are better able to do this than are the less experienced players.

Capacity restrains chess players' recall and thus also limits the representing of chess positions. Even the impairment of performance in visual secondary tasks conditions supports the argument linking capacity to the incidence of errors. The secondary tasks cause deterioration in performance and this means that capacity limits also cause errors. The limited-capacity thesis is also in accordance with the general theory of thought errors (Anderson *et al.* 1984, Johnson-Laird 1983).

Long-term memory seems to have very different functions as compared with the working memory. It provides the storage medium for a very large task-specific retrieval structure (Ericsson and Kintsch 1994). This structure is essential in the maintenance of ongoing activity; thought information very probably is not actively processed in the retrieval structure. It also seems that chess players are not aware of the contents of the retrieval structure without first retrieving it from long-term memory.

The retrieval structure contains task-relevant information. It is a part of long-term memory. Its structure entails relevant information of very different types. It begins with pieces and their visual properties and locations. It contains chess-specific relations, which associate the pieces into chunks. However, the retrieval structure seems to contain highly verbal elements. Thus the retrieval structure is a very complicated, hierarchical unit activated for some task maintenance purposes.

The construction of a retrieval structure and information access from it presupposes matching and associative processes. If the locations in the presented stimuli are transformed, subjects immediately have problems with constructing the retrieval structure. On the other hand, even a high-level cue seems to aid information coding and access (Cooke *et al.* 1993).

Co-operation between memory systems is a particularly interesting property of theirs, because it controls information selection in thinking. The contents of the working memory are probably the active and conscious part of the representation. Chess players can relate the contents of their working memories but are less well aware of the alternative non-active long-term memory information contents (cf. de Groot 1965). Thus the memory systems are strongly involved in information activation and inactivation during thinking and they have a major role in selective thinking.

The 'capacity paradox' of chess experts' memory depicts very well the task sharing between the two memory systems. The blindfold chess experiments have shown that chess experts can follow some ten simultaneous games and remember them afterwards. The memory load is very high in these experiments and it may appear very difficult to assume that chess players could not remember what they should do when searching for a move. How is it possible that a memory that can store ten simultaneous games which have been read reasonably fast may be unable to represent a solution that is two moves long?

The answer is, fortunately, simple. We use working memory to manipulate information and the limitations concern mainly this part of the representation. Long-term memory is used to store important manipulation results and alternative hypotheses, but the actual simulation of the world takes place in working memory. This is why working memory capacity is essential in explaining errors, though it is much smaller than the capacity needed in blindfold chess.

Memory systems offer several functions that are important in selective thinking, but the most essential aspects of selectivity seem to be beyond the current memory research. It cannot explain much about the selection of content-specific information and thus the content-specific aspects of selective thinking. The attributes of memory research, which very strongly rely on capacity, are not effective when content-specific information selection should be discussed.

A concrete example might clarify the above point. The mental transformation cannot be explained in terms of visual imagery or visual working memory only. The use of imagery must be conceptually and propositionally controlled. There is no imagery-level structure that could explain why a bishop is placed on the square b5 instead of c4. Thus the conceptual representation must control the contents of mental imagery (Bachmann and Oit 1992, Saariluoma 1991a). The contents of images are no longer effectively expressible in imagery research, because imagery is not a content-specific concept.

A very similar argument is true of information activation. Central executive and other corresponding systems that carry out information transfer between working memory and long-term memory are currently not content specific. No theory exists about the role of information contents in information activation. The idea of activation as well as the idea of memory are both currently content-free concepts.

This means that if we are to find ways in which to derive genuine content-specific explanations, it is necessary to study the contents of processed information directly. Though many important aspects of information encoding in selective thinking can be learned by studying memory systems, only research into the contents of information and the processes that produce these contents can provide us with information about the highest forms of selectivity.

The problem with the current concepts of experts' memory is evident. They do not have content-specific attributes. Retrieval structures are undoubtedly content-specific structures in which some relevant elements are associated. However, we have no knowledge about these content-specific aspects of memory structures, except perhaps in the research into semantic memory.

Even if we had, it is unclear what the role of memory would be in associating just the right elements together. It seems likely that thinking first creates a content-specific conceptual structure and after that these structures are stored in memory. They slowly grow in size and this enables experts to construct large representations when necessary. Nevertheless, to understand the construction process, we must turn our attention from memory to thinking.

THE PROBLEM OF FOUR CAPACITIES

One final question was pointed out to me by Robert Logie (personal communication). This is the difference between attentional and working memory capacities. How can we explain the fact that capacity is divided into two? Do these capacities have the same origin and, if not, how are they related to each other? These questions raise interesting problems concerning the notion of capacity itself, but it seems to me now that data from various chess experiments make the issue a little more complicated, because they suggest four different capacities instead of one.

Attentional capacity is normally 1 unit. If no overlapping processing resources are required and the secondary tasks are well automatized, more than one task can be carried out simultaneously. In any case attentional capacity is small. Indeed it is the smallest of the four capacities that can be found in chess players' information processing (Saariluoma 1984, 1985).

The second capacity is the one that can be found in working memory experiments. This second capacity is around 4 units, a conclusion based on the observation that novices are able to recall some four pieces. This capacity is also something that can be affected by concurrent visuo-spatial interference tasks in blindfold chess experiments (Saariluoma 1989, 1991a).

The third capacity is the skilled memory capacity or the active long-term memory capacity (Chase and Ericsson 1981, 1982, Ericsson and Kintsch 1994). By this is meant all the information in long-term memory that is actively involved in maintaining the performance of a task and for a skilled chess retrieval structure (e.g. Ericsson and Kintsch 1994). Characteristically, this memory representation cannot be disrupted by the same secondary tasks as those that affect working memory. Only an increasing memory load seems to cause problems as the representations grow too large. In blindfold chess, for example, subsequent secondary task interference does not cause much of a problem for the experts (Saariluoma 1989). Only concurrent interference causes impairment. However, the capacity of the skilled memory is not infinite, because there is a limit as to how many simultaneous games chess players are able to keep in mind. Moreover, the increasing memory load with the increasing number of moves in blindfold games causes gradual impairment in the precision of recall with medium-level players (Ericsson and Kintsch 1994, Saariluoma 1989).

The last of the four capacities is the long-term memory capacity. Chess masters seem to be able to learn some 100,000 chess patterns, at least, during a period of some ten years (Chase and Simon 1973b, Simon and Gilmartin 1973). This means that the total capacity of the long-term memory is much larger than the capacity of the skilled memory. So this total capacity of human memory is the last of the capacities. Of course, no clear limit for long-term learning can be shown.

We do not know very much about these four capacities. We do not know their origin or precise neurophysiological basis. We do not know if they are as qualitatively different as they appear to be or if they are stages in a continuum. Yet they are interesting when the concept of capacity is considered.

In practical psychology capacity is a very useful concept. Performance capacity is something we can measure and in this way it is a very important property of capacity. Psychologists must often try to assess human performance in order to adapt people to various task demands and to design psychologically more rational environments. In this kind of work capacity is a very important notion as it provides a direct measure for human capability to act in an environment.

Theoretically the notion of capacity is much more problematic, because psychologists should find explanations for the capacity phenomena. They should be able to say why people have limited capacity or relatively limited capacities. In this task it is not enough to say that we have a certain capacity; we should pinpoint the psychological structures or processes that explain the limited capacity.

Another important problem is to understand how the four capacities are related to the contents of thought. Of course, capacity can provide no ultimate answers, because the same capacity can be filled with an infinite number of contents. In any case, attention provides information about the absolute centre of stimulus processing. Working memory seems to store information that must be manipulated. Skilled memory contains information that is not actively manipulated but is necessary for solving the current problem. Finally, long-term memory contains all potentially usable task-specific knowledge. Undoubtedly future research will reveal the functions of the four capacities in maintaining thought.

Chapter 5

Apperception

In any science there are areas that the established theoretical concepts of the science cannot cover. For example, natural numbers could not express the ratio of the radius and the circumference of a circle. To express that ratio it was necessary to construct a new number concept. Similarly, in psychology new types of conceptual tools must be developed when the standard concepts are unable to express essential aspects of mind. Indeed, such tools were produced very actively in the 1960s when the current conceptual system of cognitive psychology was being developed. There is nothing exceptional in introducing new concepts and it is naturally a task for conceptual analysis.

The concepts of attention and memory can answer some but not all of the important questions in our attempts to understand selectivity in thinking. In practice, both notions are very strongly capacity oriented and thus are not able to explain why our thoughts have a certain content. Capacity does not have suitable attributes for handling content-specific questions. We think what we think independently of the capacity. The same capacity is used in any task environment and in solving any problem in these task environments. This means that capacity cannot make any difference between the contents of thoughts. In other words, capacity is not a content-specific concept or that content is not an attribute of capacity.

Capacity can explain how we can keep in mind complex cognitive structures. Our working memory cannot actively process infinitely large representations. On the contrary, the representations are quite small in size. Capacity can explain why selective information processing is necessary. It is necessary because we can attend to the world in only one way at a time. What capacity cannot express is the contents of these representations and therefore the psychological problems of contents require a new vocabulary, conceptual system and theoretical foundations. They require the development of a content-specific cognitive psychology (Allport 1980a, b).

By a content-specific cognitive psychology I mean a theory that explains human behaviour in terms of the contents of the required representations and processes needed in constructing these representations. In the psychology of selective thinking this means that psychology should explain why thoughts have a definite set of elements linked into a whole and why some other apparently equally possible set of elements is inappropriate and not included in the representation. Thus content-specific cognitive psychology is about the semantic structure or simply the contents of the representations.

Capacity-oriented cognitive psychology makes one important assumption: human mind has a measurable capacity. Thus it studies mind as a limited-capacity system. All its experiments are constructed to find attributes of capacity and the theoretical concepts are built around the notion of capacity. Typical examples are list learning or a limited-capacity channel. By restricting itself to capacity, this part of cognitive psychology has made tremendous progress and dramatically improved our understanding of mind during the past four decades; but capacity cannot help psychology to make progress in analysing the contents of mind. To analyse the contents a new 'Cartesian point' or a new ground concept must be found.

The new ground concept or conceptual postulate used to analyse 'meaningful' systems is the self-consistency of representations. Everyone knows that the human mind is highly economic in representing reality. Human representations seldom contain more than essential elements. The organization of representations is also highly consistent. The elements seem to be linked to one another in a logical fashion. The presence of each element in a representation makes sense. This means that for each element in a representation, in principle there is a reason why it belongs to this particular representation. In addition, for each element that is not in the representations but which belongs to the representations of the same task environment it should be possible to say why they do not belong to a particular representation. For this kind of self-consistent internal organization of the representations, I shall adopt the technical term *senseful*. I take the sensefulness of representations as a basic postulate for content-specific cognitive psychology in the same way that capacity is a basic postulate in capacity-oriented cognitive psychology (Broadbent 1958). This means that I study representations assuming that they have a senseful structure.

The term senseful might at first sound strange and it requires some clarification. According to the *Oxford English Dictionary* the term was used in seventeenth-century English but has not been used since, and it seems to avoid problematic connotations. It is meant to be a translation for a Finnish term *mielekäs*, which can be used to refer to senseful wholes. Normally, in scientific English a chess move, for example, is said to be 'meaningful', in quotation marks, in order to express the fact that the move makes sense in the current situation. However, scientific terms in quotation marks are vague and should be abolished. Also, it is pointless to say that the interrepresentational consistency relations are 'meaningful' since chess moves, for example, do not have any meaning at all. They simply do not refer to anything outside themselves, nor do they have any symbolic value. Finally, a basic theoretical term must be unambiguous and this is why it is best to adopt sensefulness as a technical expression.

A fundamental problem for psychology is how chess players' thoughts acquire their self-consistent and senseful structure. How does each element make sense? What kind of principles does the mind use in abstracting from huge networks of moves just the ones that make sense, or the moves that fit together? How is the mind able to neglect all of the irrelevant moves? How is the mind able to differentiate the essential and the inessential, which Dreyfus (1972) saw as the basic problem in the field? For these and similar questions, capacity-oriented psychology can provide no answer.

What kind of perception is chess players' 'seeing'? Chess players' thinking can be studied by collecting think-aloud protocols (Ericsson and Simon 1980, 1984). When chess players think aloud throughout a game or a chess problem, a reasonable picture of the contents of their thoughts can be obtained from their recorded speech (Gilhooly 1986, de Groot 1965, Newell and Simon 1972). Research into chess protocols has shown that even experts are normally content with relatively small representations. Chess players simply 'see' the essential in the positions (de Groot 1965, Newell and Simon 1972).

To understand chess players' selective thinking one must understand what is meant by 'seeing' in this context. Unfortunately, the term is problematic. No one has been able to define precisely what is meant by the term 'see'. The use of quotation marks means *de facto* the acknowledgement of the difficulties. Does 'seeing' refer to perception, attention or something else? Very probably something else, because otherwise these standard terms would have been used. To find the meaning of the term 'see', conceptual analysis is required.

The term 'see' occurs commonly in chess players' lay psychology, as in the following example:

> It is most important that we [i.e. chess players] should *see* [Golz and Keres's emphasis] with our eyes. If only we had the eyes of Argus! Yet even that hundred eyed monster . . . was taken in by one of Zeus's tricks. . . . In any case don't be taken in by appearances, don't underestimate your opponent, look at the situation objectively.
>
> (Golz and Keres 1989)

This passage shows how de Groot (1965, 1966) adopted the theoretical term 'see' from normal chess jargon, and subsequently it has been widely adopted in the literature on the psychology of expertise. There is nothing wrong in borrowing everyday terms when developing jargon, but the term 'see' has no clear meaning apart from a vague reference to perceptual experience which should go beyond 'appearances'.

As argued above, there are a number of reasons why chess players' 'seeing' cannot be interpreted as object perception or attending. Chess players' 'seeing' is not modality specific; chess players may 'see' visually and auditorily presented chess positions equally well. Blind chess players may even rely on their tactual sense in order to 'see'. The important role of imagery mediation also argues against the idea of 'seeing' as object perception and attention.

The contents of 'seeing' are also relatively independent of the stimulus content. Chess players are not allowed to move pieces but they still 'see' moves that are several plies from the original position. Individual differences in skill also affect the representational contents of 'seeing' despite the fact that the physical stimulus is the same for all. Moreover, an individual's way of 'seeing' a chess position constantly changes even although the position remains the same. The arguments against taking 'seeing' as object perception or attention are very strong; certainly it would be an oversimplification to think that chess players' 'seeing' could be equivalent to object perception.

If 'seeing' cannot be perception, what is it? What theoretical term should we use to replace this mystical and ambiguous term 'see'? There seems to be a black hole among the theoretical concepts of cognitive psychology. None of the major theoretical terms covers the 'seeing' of chess players and if the normal vocabulary could offer an alternative, why has this ambiguous expression been so popular? The reason must be that the concept behind the term 'see' intuitively is felt to be important but no one has been able to make the intuitions explicit. Paradoxically, the history of psychology contains the right answer.

The ambiguous term 'see' should be replaced by the classic term apperception, which, unlike most of the important pre-behaviouristic theoretical concepts, has not been rehabilitated (Kant 1781, Leibniz 1704, Stout 1896, Wundt 1880). Apperception refers to conceptual perception or construction of semantic representations. It is the process that forms the semantic figure of thought. It assimilates the perceptual stimulus and conceptual memory information into a semantically self-consistent representation that is characteristic of the human mind.

The semantic figure of thought comprises the contents of mental representations. I may sit in my office and look out of the window while thinking about Galileo's experiments with falling bodies. The contents of my mind have nothing to do with the perceived environment. The focus of my thoughts is thousands of kilometres and hundred of years away from my visible environment. The semantic figure of my thought may move from the concrete tower of Pisa to Galileo's abstract concept of time. To control the movement of the contents of my representations, I need to have a cognitive process, which is responsible for it. This process is apperception.

It is important to understand that apperception is a content-specific process. Apperception determines which semantic elements of conceptual memory and of the stimulus information can be and should be assimilated into one single representation. Apperception is also the mechanism which can carry out the process of synthesizing the two types of representational contents into one representation, and thus apperception determines the semantic structure of representations.

Apperception provides representations with their senseful structure. The contents of apperceived representations need not be directly related to the stimulus environment. The main issue is that the apperceived representations are self-consistent. They do not have senseless content elements. They may be false or true, but they must be consistent.

The research into apperception in chess should thus concentrate on the semantic relations between representational elements, i.e. moves, combinations and strategic elements. The selection and organization of the content-specific elements is the research problem for apperception research. The point of view should be content-specific, because apperception is about the contents of information in mind. This means also that the explanations should be based on these contents of the elements. Only in this way may we improve our understanding of the synthesizing operations in mind.

TWO TASK-ENVIRONMENTAL LEVELS OF PROBLEM TREES

Content-specific cognitive psychology begins with the analysis of the semantic structure of the environment. The contents of mind must follow the structure of environment. Rational thinking involves understanding the environment, and thus the contents of thoughts must follow the structure and contents of environment. Apperception may construct senseful representations only if it abstracts the environment in an appropriate way. Therefore it is not possible to study apperception or any content-specific process without first analysing the environment.

As discussed earlier chess, like most games, has a tree structure. However, this tree structure contains several levels and thus it is necessary to make the prevailing language less ambiguous by sharpening the terminology of Newell and Simon (1972). Otherwise, it is not possible to express precisely how mind follows the environment.

The total game tree of chess, which begins from the initial position and ends with the terminal nodes of all possible branches of the game tree of chess, should be called the total problem space of chess. Its subtrees individuated by any position in the total problem space which is not the initial position can be termed the basic problem space.

The total problem space and the basic problem space are objective, and thus they do not depend on the wishes or will of the players. Chess positions are what they are, and when a player tries to search for a move he or she must find the solution in the conditions of the current position. Only new moves may change the situation, but then also the basic problem space is new.

MENTAL REPRESENTATIONS

Both total and basic problem spaces are represented intensionally or implicitly in chess players' minds. They are intensionally represented because the initial position and the movement rules allow players, in principle, to generate all the possible paths of these trees. However, total problem space and very often also the positions of basic problem spaces are not presentable because no one can, in practice, generate all the moves. Total and basic problem spaces are thus not extensionally representable.

It is important to understand that only extensionally representable sets of positions and subtrees have real significance in chess players' thinking. Chess players have no opportunity to test their ideas unless they are able to generate the positions of the subtree between the initial position and the goal positions. Consequently, the total problem space and the basic problem spaces are only of secondary importance in psychological research and the main focus must be on the mental representations.

Apperception can be characterized as the process that creates senseful representations in mind. Though this definition is correct and sufficiently general, it is necessary to define precisely what the senseful representations are like in each task environment. The reason is simple. Sensefulness depends on the contents of mind. This is why the way mind represents any particular environment must be studied separately.

In chess, the general levels of mental representing can be found by analysing the search tree in the protocols (de Groot 1965, Newell and Simon 1972). The search tree containing all the moves generated by a subject when searching for a solution could be termed the subjective search space. The subjective search space comprises all the moves, positions and paths represented in the mind of a chess player during the time he or she is solving a problem. The name subjective search space can be justified by its subjective character. The subjective search space depends on individual chess players' minds. Their learning, skill, stylistic preferences, etc. affect the form of the subjective search space.

Though subjective search spaces contain all the moves found by

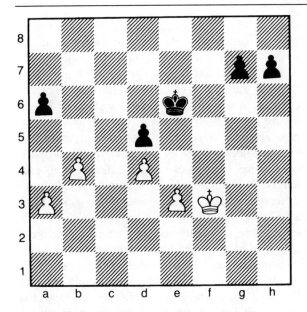

(Ep1) King, if 1. e4 then 1. –, d takes e4, 2. king takes e4. After that two connected passed pawns decide. (Ep2) 1. a4 g5, 2. b5 a × b5. 3. a5 Kd6, 4. a6 Kc6 and the king reaches the square. (Ep3) 1. a4 g5, 2. Kg4 h6, forced. From the beginning (Ep4) 1. a4, h5, 2. Kf4 Kf6. If 3. –, Kf6, then 4. b5 and the king is no longer in the square. (Ep5) So, White moves 1. a4. If 1. –, h5 then 2. Kf4. If 1. –, g5 then 2. Kg4. (Ep6) So, 1. a4 h5, 2. Kf4 h4, king . . . no king . . . yes 3. Kg4 g5, 4. b5 a takes b, 5. –, Kd6, 6. Kh3 Kc7. This does not work. (Ep7) 1. a4 h5, 2. Kf4 h4. No. (Ep8). The first move must be be 1. e4. If does not take then 2. e5 and protected passed pawn. 1. –, d-pawn takes, 2. king takes back, h5, 3. a4 g5, 4. b5 a takes, 5. –, Kd6. It does not work in this way either. (Ep9) 1. a4 h5, 2. Kf4 h4. (Ep10) No . . . 1. a4 h5, 2. Kf4 h4, 3. e4, d takes e, 4. b5 a takes b, 5. a5, but Kd6, 6. a6, Kc6, 7. d5; if 7. –, Kb6 then 8. d6. Cannot stop both and the counter-action is too late. I play 1. a4.

Figure 5.1 A protocol: the beginnings of episodes are marked with Ep and a number

chess players when solving a problem, it is not the best basic unit for a psychological analysis of apperception in chess players' thinking. The reason is that subjective search spaces contain several logically structured but mutually opposite elements.

Protocols are normally discontinuous. They have an episodic

structure (de Groot 1965, Newell and Simon 1972). Episodes usually begin with a base move – that is, a move made in the initial position – and contain a number of moves ending up at a possible terminal or goal position. Though episodes often refer to very similar ideas, they may also have very different contents.

Usually the contents of a part of the episodes are very closely linked. They may, for example, have several common moves in the beginning. If these episodes were united into a single tree, they would make a very logical subtree of the basic problem space. Equally commonly, some episodes are very different from each other. They have no common moves in the beginning and the goals are also very different. Whereas one episode may win a pawn another may end in mate.

Closely related episodes normally seem to refer to a common idea. This idea is a kind of deep structure behind several episodes. This common problem subspace which associates several episodes, I call here mental space. Mental space contains a single logically consistent small search tree, which is a subspace of subjective search space. Since mental spaces are logically consistent wholes, it is natural to take them as the basic unit in the cognitive analysis of apperception and thinking in chess (Saariluoma 1984). These sub-trees of subjective search trees make up the core of chess players' thinking. The term mental space is justified since mental spaces are temporary mental representations of problem positions. Figure 5.2 presents subjective search space with mental spaces corresponding to the protocol in Figure 5.1. One should observe that several episodes may refer to one and the same mental space.

Ms1. e4 d × e4, K × e4 h5, a4 g5, b5 a × b5 a × b5 Kd6
        ---, e5
Ms2. a4 g5, b5 a × b5, a5 Kd6, a6 Kc6, Kg4 h6

Ms3. a4 h5, Kf4 h4, e4 d × e4, b5 a × b5, a5 Kd6, a6 Kc6, d5 Kb6, d6 Kf6, d5

Figure 5.2 Subjective search space and three mental spaces in the protocol of Figure 5.1. Mental space 3 (Ms3) is a combination of Ms1 and Ms2. In this figure all but the moves are abstracted from a protocol. This kind of description is termed problem behaviour graph
Source: Newell and Simon (1972)

(1) Total problem space: the game tree, the root of which is the initial position and which contains all the legal moves.
(2) Basic problem space: the game tree which has its root in any chess position and which contains all legal moves from the root onwards.
(3) Subjective search space: the game tree that contains all moves generated in a protocol.
(4) Mental space: a game tree that contains a set of logically linked moves.

Figure 5.3 The types of problem spaces

Mental spaces are trees of logically consistent moves. Each move has a function in the total structure of a mental space. Subjects can find a solution even though they might be unable to see any of the mental spaces other than the one that contains the solution. The different mental spaces are not usually connected logically. They are, in fact, in semantic opposition and as such they cannot be unified. For example, the same piece may be in two different squares at the same time in the different mental spaces. Sometimes mental spaces contain null moves, but this does not change their structural principles (de Groot 1965, Hohlfeld 1988, Newell and Simon 1972, Saariluoma 1992b).

Mental spaces are constructed by apperceptive processes. Apperception gives mental spaces their logically consistent structure. This logic follows the structure of basic problem space, but a mental space is highly selected and the selection process depends on apperception. Thus the analysis of mental spaces may also reveal the principles of apperception.

The total and basic problem spaces are objective. Subjective search spaces and mental spaces are subjective (Figure 5.3). They depend on the mind of the players and their generation follows the principles of the human mind. What a mental space and subjective search space consist of depends on a player's ability. Experts generate mental spaces with more adequate contents than novices.

The basic problem spaces provide the ultimate measure for the correctness of a mental space. This means that a mental space is rational only if it provides a true representation of the possibilities in the corresponding basic problem space.

THE LOGIC OF DEFENDERS' MOVES

Apperceiving is the organizing of the mental representations by their contents, and apperception research which takes the sensefulness of representations as its basic assumption concentrates just on this aspect of mental spaces. The senseful organization of a mental representation means that all elements of the representation have some reason to be embraced by the representation.

In chess, this means that we must analyse precisely why the moves which belong to the representation are parts of the representation instead of all the other equally legal moves. The crucial question is: what kind of content-specific principles and mechanisms are employed by apperception to control the information selection in the construction of mental spaces?

Apperceived moves – that is, the moves in a mental space – cannot be accidental; they must have some internal connections that make the mental spaces self-consistent and senseful wholes. Chess players' generation of a mental space is not a blind trial-and-error process; the moves make up a senseful system. If the search were casual, the moves in the protocols would be much more random. The problem is to find the principles that apperception uses in selecting the relevant moves from all possible moves.

Saariluoma (1990b) investigated and demonstrated some essential factors that explain the self-consistency of mental spaces. In these experiments chess combinations were presented to the subjects and think-aloud protocols were collected. Figure 5.4 presents one example of a similar experiment.

The main problem is: what controls the generation of new move sequences? There are millions of alternative paths to those found in the protocols. Why are just these moves mentally generated? There must be a content-specific control mechanism to explain the selection of moves. To uncover the secrets of the content-specific selection of moves it is best to concentrate first on the defender's moves, because the principles on which these moves are based are relatively simple.

In the current position (Figure 5.4), White's attack moves R × g7, Qg2, Nf7 or R × g7, Qd5, Nd7, N × f6 form a path for the attacker from the initial position to a set of good goal positions. Black has to try to prevent White from achieving this goal, because it would be a mate or very serious loss of material and mean the loss of the game. Hence all Black's moves have one goal: preventing White from executing the planned series of moves. If we could find the principles behind Black's moves, this would yield the first idea about the content-specific control of mental move generation and the sensefulness of apperception.

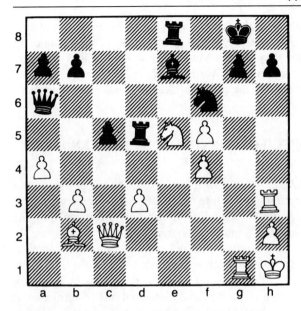

Ms: R × g7+ K × g7, Qg2+ Kh8, Nf7
                           Kf8, Qg5 null, Qh6
                                 R × h7 N × h7, Q × d5 null, Qf7 mate
                                              Qf6, Nd7+ null, N × f6
                                              Kg7, Qf7+ Kh6, Ng4 mate

Figure 5.4 Senseful structure of a mental space

The logic of the defender's moves is crucial for the whole theory of apperception and mental space abstraction presented here. If no sense can be found in Black's moves, the theory must be abandoned. Can Black's moves have any senseful connection with White's moves? Do the relevant moves have any common denominator or denominators that would make their selection more probable than the selection of some other move? Why would no one try b6 after R × g7, for example? Why do moves other than those in the protocols look totally senseless? The answer to these questions is decisive.

The core of the problem seems to be in the content-specific constraints that control move selection. We must understand what separates senseful moves from senseless. Let us thus concentrate on Figure 5.4 and continue the analysis. Moves such as b6 cannot in any way interfere with White's intention to checkmate on g7. They are too far away from the attacker's path, they do not have any

connection with White's actions, and they just do not lead to a
suitable path generated by White. Consequently, they cannot be
relevant because they cannot prevent White from achieving his or
her goal. This suggests that we must concentrate on the content-
specific constraints for the moves which may end up in the attacker's path.

CONTENT-SPECIFIC CONSTRAINTS OF DEFENDERS' MOVES

A subsequent question can now be raised: what kind of moves can,
in principle, interfere with White's attack and thus be relevant? One
criterion is obvious: the move must end by obstructing the path
defined by the attacker's moves. The term 'attacker' means here the
side which has the initiative, or which can determine the course of
play. The squares on which active supporting pieces are located are
also important (e.g. the bishop on b2 and and the rook on h3). Thus
in the above position (Figure 5.4), a move that has no influence on
the path squares such as g2, g7, f7, etc. is not efficient.

However, only some of the theoretically important squares are
relevant, because, in practice, Black cannot meet the attack on any
path square. Black is unable to move a piece to any of the critical
path squares. If the black rook were on d7 instead of d5, Black could
prevent the plan by taking with his knight the rook on h7, and this
would be a reasonable move. Now Black loses, because the queen
can take the rook on d5.

It seems that almost all the moves which can end up in the
defender's path belong to four major categories. They are
exchange, blockade, escape and counter-action moves (Saariluoma
1990b). More categories can be presented, but they seem to be of
much less significance than these four main move types. In the
above position, for example, the four more types, which will be
defined below, are sufficient for explaining all the moves generated
by the defender.

The first category of defender's senseful moves comprises
exchange moves. They are moves that exchange one of the attacker's path pieces or threaten to exchange it if it goes to a path square.
These two cases, real exchange or imagined exchange, can be taken
as equivalent, because the calculation of variations takes place
inside one's head and no real moves are made. So in the case
where the defender places his knight so that it can take the attack-

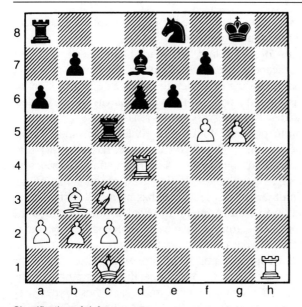

Classification of defence moves
Mental space 1:
f6 R × g5 (exchange), Rdh4 Kf8 (escape), Rh8 Rg8 (blockade)
Mental space 2:
Nd5 e × d5 (exchange), f6 and Rd4–h8 mates. No effective defence moves can be found.

Figure 5.5 An example of three of the four principles of mental space construction for the defence

er's queen, whether the attacker avoids the threat or does not makes no difference as far as the logic of mental spaces is concerned. In the example K × g7 or Qf6 are typical attempts to exchange one of the attacker's key pieces.

The second defender's move type is blockade. By blockade I refer to the placing of a piece on a square which an opponent's piece must pass, but on which it normally would not stop. A special case of blockade takes place, when, for example, the king is moved in front of a pawn to prevent it from being promoted. Blockade can sometimes lead to exchanges, because in many variations the blockading piece could be taken. The crucial difference is in the blockade square. No opponent's piece is aiming to stop on this square, only to pass it. Exchange always takes place on a square where the piece stays or where it is intended to move the piece. Blockade takes place on some of the intervening squares.

A third means of defending is escape. The move Kf8, for example, is an escape move. The escape of the target is a very common method of fending off a plan in the case of an attack on the king, but it is also found when other pieces or pawns are concerned. Only empty squares cannot escape when attacked.

Finally, a fourth principle followed by the players in selecting moves is counter-action. If White, for example, has a mating plan that can be realized in four moves, but Black finds a means to checkmate White in two moves, White must abandon his or her plan, at least temporarily. Also, if White has nothing forcing Black, then Black is allowed to play freely. Counter-action is perhaps the most difficult of all the four principles to define precisely, but it cannot be omitted. It is an essential part of chess.

An immediate example might be illuminating (Figure 5.5). The defender's move types define content-specific constraints for the generation of defender's moves. Only moves of these types may make sense in trying to parry the attack, and all the subjects in all protocols generate moves drawn from these four types for their defence. It means that these four constraints on the path explain the senseful structure of mental spaces in protocols. Even more, the move types explain also the size of mental spaces. In practice, only a few moves may fulfil one of these criteria, and this is why the mental spaces are so compact (Saariluoma 1990b).

Apperception relies thus on very simple content-specific principles in selecting defender's moves. However, merely by applying these few constraints a player is able in his or her thinking to filter sensible-sized sets of defender's moves out of millions of alternative move paths. These first findings also give us the first glimpse of the power of apperceptive processes.

THE LOGIC OF THE ATTACKER'S PATH

The four defender's principles just discussed, i.e. exchange, blockade, escape and counter-action, explain a great deal about a human chess player's search from the defender's point of view, but the attacker's move sequences are just as controlled as the defender's moves. The moves in protocols are clearly mere fragments of all possible move sequences, and this means that they must also follow some internal logic. A part of the solution can be found in the recognition and generation of associated moves (Chase and Simon 1973b). When chess players recognize a familiar combination, they can instantly generate some relevant moves. The problem is that recognition is not an explanation of the internal logic of the generated moves. Recognition–association theory merely says that people recognize familiar patterns; it has nothing to say about the organization of the moves in the generated move patterns. If no content-specific control existed, the moves could be legal, but selected at random. This means that the generated move sequences, searched or recognized, must make sense. The solution to the attacker's move control problem is analogous to the solution associated with control of the defender's moves. The attacker is always attacking something, either a specific square or a small set of specific squares. These squares and the pieces in these squares respectively I call target squares and targets. The square(s) in which the target is located can be called a target square. In terms of the functional structure of a mental space, the target square is the most vital square on the board. The attacker must get some piece on to that square to reach the goal, and therefore the target square spans the attacker's path and the whole mental space.

Let us assume that this target is the king. In a normal chess position the king can be threatened by only a few pieces, if it can be threatened at all. These pieces cannot threaten the king from any square, they can only attack the king from a few squares. Let us term these squares 'key squares'. To threaten the king, a piece must be able to move into a key square. In practice, the attacker's pieces do not have unlimited opportunities to do so. The key squares must be free for the attacker's pieces, and typically the number of such squares is small. (Figure 5.6 serves to illustrate these points.)

The target and key squares help us now to derive a classification scheme for the attacker's moves which is similar to that for the defender's moves, and this means that the same spatial logic controls both attackers' and defenders' moves. Let me take two examples. A move whose current end-square is not the final goal for the moving piece in the move network can be called a transfer move. A move to a key square which has the aim of occupying another square can be called a threat. Further, a transfer move which is intended as a threat, e.g. to take a piece, can be called a transfer for threat. To occupy a key square and make a threat, one must be able to transfer piece(s) into key square(s). The piece cannot, however, be transferred via squares an opponent is able to defend.

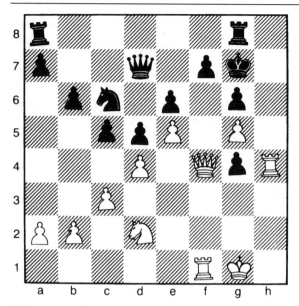

Well, this is so that . . . yes . . . Rh7+ Kf8 is impossible because White has three pieces which can take [on f7] so the only move is R × h7+ K × h7, Qh2 and Black must play Kg7, Qh6 mate.

Key squares for White h7, f7, h2, h6. The crucial key square h6.
Path squares: h3, h4, h5, g7, f7, f4, g3.

Note that, if Black had the move, the knight on d8 could support f7 and the whole combination would collapse.

Figure 5.6 Position, protocol, key squares and path

An opponent must not be able to exchange the key piece or blockade it, nor can the opponent exchange or blockade some of the supporting pieces. This means that senseful transfer moves do not have much space on a chessboard, because the key piece(s) must be transferred to the key squares along safe routes.

The location of the target thus spans the attacker's path. It determines both the possible squares for transfer and the key squares. The key square must be free or it must be freed by some preliminary operations. This means that the defender must be unable either to exchange an attacker's key piece, or to blockade the attack, and the path to the key and target square must also be free. The number of such squares and corresponding operations, i.e. moves reaching the key squares, is always very small. The pawn chain, the fields of threat of the pieces, and the location of the target greatly constrain the attacker's senseful moves. The attacker cannot reach the target squares as he or she wishes, but must instead find or create a system of weaknesses in the opponent's camp.

The same simple principles are also valid when the target is something other than the king. The target may equally well be the opponent's piece, pawn, or just an empty square. Even in restriction-type cases in which one tries to control the whole system of the opponent's squares, the control of the restricting piece must be located in a key square and the occupation of this square spans the move network in a mental space.

Human chess players' apperception follows thus in generating mental spaces by means of very simple content-specific principles. These principles explain why subjects do not generate more than ten to a hundred moves for positions in which computers would generate millions of alternatives. The principles also explain why some moves are selected and why some other moves are neglected.

The number of moves fulfilling the constraints is always very small compared to all possible moves. The whole economy of chess players' apperception is based on these very simple principles. They define what is essential and what is not in a network of moves. Neglecting one move that does not fill the content-specific constraints does not mean anything, but neglecting one relevant move may jeopardize the problem-solving process.

This description of a problem-solving process and a few content-specific principles provide an explicit definition of the concept of chess-specific sense. Moves are senseful only if they are designed to parry or to aid some operation and fill the content-specific criteria for relevant moves. Consequently, the principles presented here can be used to explain the nature of the search moves.

Interestingly, these principles are not widely known among chess players. The types of defence moves and by and large also the attacker's moves were totally unknown to me and they cannot be found in chess books. They are too primitive to have a prominent place in chess theory. Nor can they be found in protocols. Yet all chess players use them all the time when calculating variations. This means that human apperception uses unconscious or implicit primitive principles in separating the essential from the inessential. The use of unconscious content-specific principles is probably the most interesting aspect of the constraints on moves, because it raises the

Target ——————> Attacker's goal path ——————> Defender's paths

Figure 5.7 Idealized mental space construction process

question as to what degree human apperception is based on similar unconscious or tacit task-specific principles.

THE SENSEFUL STRUCTURE OF MENTAL SPACES

Apperception uses content-specific and unconscious principles to provide the mental spaces with senseful structure. Only information that fills the constraints is accepted. Thus chess players' apperception is an example of content-specific information selection in thinking. The explanation of information selection is based on the senseful structure of the representations and not capacity or some other principle.

Chess players only generate moves that make sense in the senseful structure of mental spaces and thus follow the content-specific principles that have been presented so far. It is the structure of mental spaces (see Figure 5.7) which makes content-specific selection possible, and uncovering this structure in detail is an important task for the psychology of chess skill. Many of the reasons for the consistency of mental spaces are now apparent, but much work must be done to clarify the details. A target square and a set of key squares and the supporting pieces span the attacker's critical path. In problem-solving language, the target square is the goal. If no counter-action can be found, the defender must search for moves that can intersect with the path. Only moves that will do this are relevant.

The range of types of moves spanning mental spaces found so far is relatively small. Some of them have not yet been discussed, but a set of all the principles used in this book is shown in Figure 5.8. One further remark: a move may fulfil several criteria simultaneously. It may be an escape and a threat move at the same time, for example. In fact, the most effective moves often fulfil several criteria at the same time. In this way they may turn defence into attack and thus give the opponent very little time to organize any counter-actions.

Transfer (tr) = a piece is moved to get it to the path by some subsequent move

Exchange (ex) = an active piece is taken

Blockade (blo) = an active piece is prevented from reaching a key square by placing a piece between its original square and its destination square

Escape (es) = the target piece is moved to another square

Pin (p) = an active piece is prevented from moving by placing a piece so that its movement is illegal (absolute pin) or would cost too much material (relative pin)

Unblockade (ubl) = a piece is moved to allow some other piece to make an active move

Clearange (cl) = enemy piece supporting some key square is exchanged or forced to lose the control over a key square

Decoy (dc) = a target piece is forced to move on to an unpleasant square

Threat (thr) = a piece is moved to achieve a goal in the next move

Counter-action (ca) = any move that is made to achieve some independent goal

Figure 5.8 Content-specific constraints for mental space spanning. The abbreviations will be used in the subsequent analysis

EXAMPLES OF APPERCEPTION AND MENTAL SPACES IN MIDDLE GAME POSITIONS

To provide readers with a better idea about the abstraction of mental spaces it is necessary to present concrete examples and analyse them in detail. Work with mental spaces is a relatively, but not totally, mechanical operation, and therefore one must have some experience about the contents of the protocols. To study apperception, it is necessary to understand what subjects say in the protocols. The general principles are not sufficient alone, for a researcher must have practical examples and experience of how these principles are applied.

I shall first take two very simple examples. They are a position from Newell and Simon (1972), which is the finale of the 'Immortal' game Andersen v. Kieseritzky, and a position from our collection of protocols. In Figure 5.9, the path is presented first with the moves given underneath, and their classification in the column on the right-hand side. I shall concentrate on the most important move sequences only. In this example all the moves in the mental space follow the presented principles for the abstraction of mental spaces. The example is, however, quite simple, as the position is in a relatively late stage of the combination.

The next example, shown in Figure 5.10, is taken from Saari-

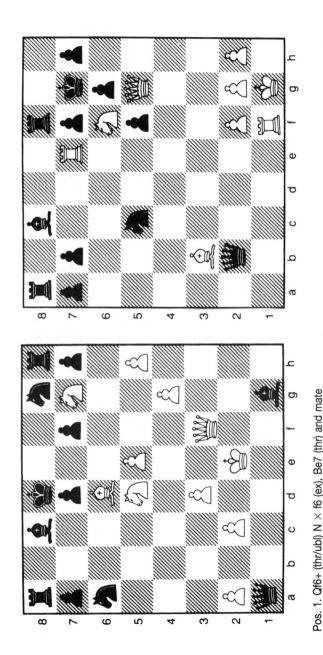

Pos. 1. Qf6+ (thr/ubl) N × f6 (ex), Be7 (thr) and mate
Pos. 2. R × f7 (thr) R × f7 (ex), Nh5+ (thr) Kf8 (esc), Qd8 mate
                                 Kg8 (esc), Qd8 mate
                                 Kh8 (esc), Qd8 (thr) Rf8 (blo), Q × f8

Figure 5.9 Two examples of the move classification. (For the system of abbreviations see Figure 5.8)

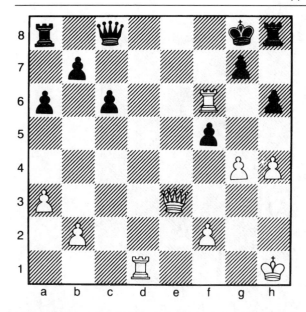

Rd8+ (thr/cl) Q × d8 (ex), Qe6+ (thr) Kh7 (esc), R × h6 (thr/cl) g × h6 (ex), Qf7 mate

Figure 5.10 A more complex example

luoma (1984). It is more complicated than the previous example, but the same principles will be applied in its analysis. The path spanned by the target square directs the search and abstraction of mental spaces.

The third example (Figure 5.11) is even more complicated. It is Paul Keres's protocol from de Groot's (1965) famous position A.

All three examples show that there is no difficulty in applying the presented content-specific constraints in the analysis of tactical middle game situations. The system seems to cover the normal cases very well.

EXAMPLES FROM ENDGAMES

The chess term 'endgame' refers to positions in which most of the pieces have been exchanged and the number of pieces is so small that direct assaults on the king are usually impossible. Though endgames are very different from middle games thinking in them seems to follow similar principles. Endgames form a very important

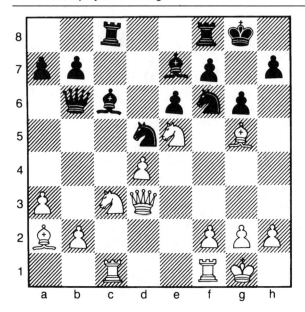

Ms1. Bh6 (thr) null, N × f7 (ex)
Ms2. N × c6 (thr/ex) b × c6 (ex), B × d5 (thr/ex) c × d5 (ex), Qf3 (thr)
Ms3. B × d5 (thr/ex) B × d5 (ex), Nd7 (thr)
                 e × d5 (ex), Qf3 (thr) Kg7 (ex), Ng4 (thr)
                 B × d5 (thr/dc) B × d5 (ex)

Figure 5.11 Paul Keres's moves
Source: de Groot (1965)

area of chess playing, and it is often said that beginners and masters differ most in this area of chess. Clearly, skilled endgame play is one of the most important requirements for high-level chess. This is why it is necessary to study apperceptive processes and the logic of subspaces also with endgame positions.

Figure 5.12 presents an endgame protocol, which is different from the middle game positions that we have studied so far. Nevertheless the same principles are still valid. This is no surprise. In chess, all that is acquired must be gained by moving pieces through a set of squares. If the opponent tries to prevent a player from mating, taking pieces, or occupying squares, this must be done on the squares through which the attacker's pieces move. It must take place on the critical path, unless a suitable counter-action can be found. The endgame is no exception.

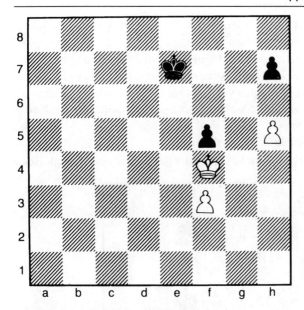

Ms1. K × f5 (ex) Kf7 (blo)
Ms2. Kg5 (tr/thr) Ke6 (blo), f4 (blo) Kf7 (blo),
     Kh6 (tr/thr) Kf6 (blo), K × h7 (ex) Kf7 (blo), h6 (tr)

Figure 5.12 Analysis of an endgame protocol

A CHESS PROBLEM

The next example is a chess problem. Chess problems are not from real games, but are composed. Pieces are placed on the board to achieve a position with particularly interesting characteristics. The goal of the problem is characterized verbally. So, for example, the solver may be told that White can checkmate in two moves, or three moves, or achieve a draw, etc. The task of the problem solver is to show how the goal can be achieved.

Chess problems provide a good environment to test the generality of presented ideas. Chess problems are different in appearance from chess positions. They do not normally have the solid pawn-chains typical of game positions. Consequently, chess players are not always particularly successful in solving them (Gruber and Strube 1989). In addition, the tactical plans are often very different from those encountered in real-game positions. Despite those differences, chess problems can be used to test the generality of the principles found in real-game problem solving.

The problem illustrated in Figure 5.13 was shown to five subjects. It was composed by a famous chess problemist, Troitsky (1968), and in it White wins through a very elegant series of moves. None of the subjects were able to solve the problem (Saariluoma 1979). Nevertheless, the protocols show that chess problems can be analysed similarly to middle game positions.

In chess problems moves are usually more or less forced. Since

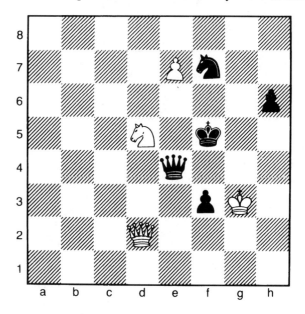

Ms1. Qe3 (thr/cl) Q × d5 (ca), e8Q (ca)
                  Q × e3 (ex), N × e3 (ex) null, e8Q (ca)
                  Nd6 (ex), Q × f3 (ex)
                  Qg4+ (ca), Kf2 (esc), Qg2+ (thr) Ke1 (es),

Qh1(thr)
Ms2. e8Q (thr) Q × e8 (ex)
Ms3. Ne3 (thr) Kg6 (es)
Ms4. Qd3 (p) Q × d3 (ex), e8Q (thr)
Solution (main line): e8Q (cl) Q × e8 (ex), Qf4+ (thr) Kg6 (es),
Qg4+ (thr) Ng5 (blo), Qh5+ (dc) K × h5 (ex), Nf4 mate

Figure 5.13 Analysis of a chess problem protocol
Source: Saariluoma (1979)

the notion of 'forcing' is important in both game positions and chess problems, it must be defined. A move is forced when one cannot find a reasonable alternative to it. In the above example all the defender's moves were forced. He had no choice but to walk into a mating net or lose a substantial number of pieces.

A forced move, like any move, is reasonable and relevant only if it fulfils the criteria presented above for mental space abstraction. Typically, forced moves always fulfil the criteria and thus the tactical positions and chess problems have a particularly forcing character. However, forced counter-action is a rarity, since counter-actions are usually voluntary.

COMBINING PLANS IN MENTAL SPACE ABSTRACTION

The previous examples are too elementary to provide the best possible insight into the complexity of apperception in chess. They are mostly exemplars with mental spaces based on a single good plan, which does not give an accurate picture of the complex-

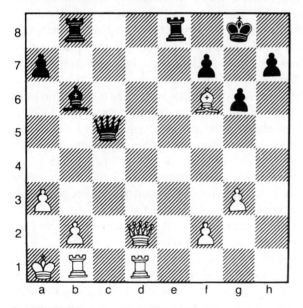

Qh6 (tr/thr) Qf8 (ex), Q × h7 (dec) K × h7 (ex), Rh1 (thr) Qh6 (blo), R × h6+ (dc) Kg8 (es), Rh8 mate

Figure 5.14 A two-theme combination

ity of chess. Chess players do not just recognize plans and apply them; instead, they painstakingly build complex mental spaces, i.e. combinations, combining or unifying several plans into a single self-consistent mental space.

The following examples are important to avoid oversimplified conceptions of apperception. Though we now understand the first principles, we have a long way to go before we can fully understand chess players' apperception. Apperception means combining any conceptual knowledge into a representation. Plans or, as chess players say, themes or motifs of combinations are also conceptual structures, and thus their association is very important.

In the experiments that follow it will be demonstrated how various plans are linked or embedded within one another to form a single self-consistent and senseful mental space. The first example is from Saariluoma (1984), and it is a simple two-theme or two prototypical problem space combination (see Figure 5.14). In this example, the subject has to apply two plans one after another. When the first plan is applied, the subject moves his queen to h5. The idea is to checkmate on g7. Black is, however, able to parry the threat and therefore White must develop an alternative plan. The new plan is to take the pawn on h7, making the attack with the bishop and the rooks. Both plans are quite straightforward, but some subjects have difficulties in combining the two plans.

The failure to combine two plans appears when a subject finds the first plan but fails to discover the second. Saariluoma (1992b) studied this phenomenon in an experiment in which he presented the subjects with six combinations having two prototypical problem spaces. In this experiment it was observed how many moves of the final solution path subjects were able to generate. The results of the experiment show how subjects usually lost the correct path when linking the two themes. The location of the major failures in the links of the combinations show how subjects really have to combine plans in order to solve this kind of problem.

The spanning of the mental space is not essentially different in the case of multiplan combinations from that in single-plan combinations. The same four principles are sufficient. The analysis in Figure 5.14 illustrates this. There is not much difference whether the active side makes threats via a path that is defined in one plan or in two. The plan comprises in any case moves that must pass and stop on certain squares, and there is no way the defending side could avoid

Chaining:
First theme (G7 mate) joins after the second plan (Rook mate).
No changes in active pieces.
Embedding:
Second plan (Nd5 blockade) is embedded into the first plan (back-row mate).
Essential changes in the active pieces.

Figure 5.15 Chaining and embedding (positions Figures 5.5 and 5.14)

the fact that these squares are precisely the squares on which the battle must be fought.

There is very little knowledge about how the plans combine in mental space abstraction. How are plans associated with each other? Saariluoma (1984) proposed two possible ways (see Figure 5.15). The first of these can be called chaining and the latter embedding. They are very probably not the only types of association, but very little is known about this important topic, and concrete empirical work is badly needed. There is no other way, when really deep knowledge about the mechanisms of chess players' thinking is required.

In chaining, the subject first follows through to the end of a mental space generated by a plan. When the player reaches the end position or some late terminal node, he or she suddenly notices that a new plan must be linked to the end of the old plan. The first plan must be linked with the second plan (Saariluoma 1984). The final mental space is therefore based on the combination of two separate plans that are spatially and temporally successive.

In the bottom part of Figure 5.15 a new type of combining can be found. The new plan, knight blockade, is not linked at the end of the variation but is embedded into its very beginning. The idea of the knight sacrifice is to blockade the defender's key piece, the rook on c5, from coming in to defend the king. De Groot (1965) would perhaps have called the rook a conflict element. The elimination of this conflict element, based on the normal principles of mental space operations, makes it possible to realize the plan.

The thought process is certainly very different from the one in the previous figure. The solution is not achieved simply by finding a new plan at the end of the first plan, but by analysing the elements of the situation in detail and embedding a new plan into the structure of the old plan.

At the moment we do not know much about combining, but it is certainly a vital problem for apperception research. The plans in a chess player's long-term memory are not always directly applicable in the positions that appear in the course of a chess game. The adaptation often requires combination, and therefore this process is important in mental space construction.

DIVERSION

The mental spaces discussed so far are elementary. More complex mental spaces require special attention, though the principles are not different. Important sources of complications may appear, when a safe goal is changed to another or when several problem subspaces are combined.

The proposed key square is not always reachable. It may be that

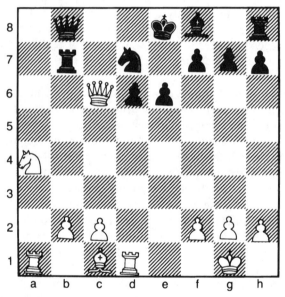

Protocol: Qc6, Rook takes d6. No. bishop and knight c5. Knight takes, Rook takes, Ra8. Knight c5 Rc7, N × d7 R × c6 N × b8. Nc7 and Rook escapes . . . yes Nc5.

Here we have a very fragmentary and messy protocol. It must be interpreted when the null moves are filled as follows: i) Nc5 d × c5, R × d7 R × d7, Ra8.

ii) Nc5 Rc7, N × d7 R × c6, N × b8. Line B is a diversion of line A. This means that Black avoids losing after d × c5, but loses after White takes another course, i.e. diverts.

Figure 5.16 Diversion

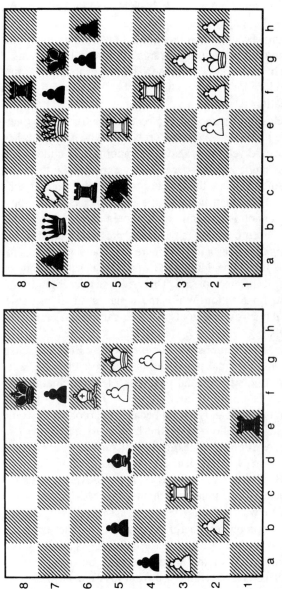

The left-hand position is a combination by Bobby Fischer. Rh3 forces Ke8 and the final blow Rd3 is now possible. The right-hand position is one of my experimental positions. Here the final mating square is g8. White's attack begins with Ne8+; if rook takes knight decisive material is lost. Kg8 is forced because the rook on f8 would be otherwise lost. Nf6+ and the king must come to g7 to protect the rook. Again, rook takes f6 loses material. After Kg7 the first pregame is over. Now the decisive combination may begin. Q × f8+ K × f8 Re8+ Kg7, and Rg8 mate. Several diversion possibilities existed, but none of them was satisfactory from Black's point of view.

Figure 5.17 Two pregames

the initial key square can be defended so that the original goal cannot be reached. The defence may also have difficulties, because moving a defending piece decreases its ability to control some other square. Sometimes some other square is weakened instead, and the key square and the target can be changed. This kind of goal transformation process I term 'diversion'. Diversion is a process that is of real interest in future research. Figure 5.16 presents a protocol in which diversion takes place. The player thinks first that he or she should follow continuation A, but subsequently turns attention to variation B.

Diversion is close to restructuring (see Chapter 6), because new episodes may be based on goal transformation, which is typical of diversion. However, diversion is also very important for understanding the logic of a single mental space. It may explain how the focus is first on some square so that the attacker puts pressure on it and the defender defends it, and then suddenly the attack breaks out on some other square. Diversion is also important in pregames (Figure 5.17).

Diversion is the core of pregames. The pregame includes any preparatory action that frees a target square or some path squares for the overt action. In the beginning the final target square may be attacked by several different pieces. This is the case in Figure 5.17. To carry out the final action White must play a small pregame. Actions against the subsidiary goals must be carried out before the final blow at square g8.

The first of the two positions is a combination by Bobby Fischer. Rh3 forces Ke8 and the final blow Rd3 is now possible. The latter position is one of my experimental positions. Here the final mating square is g8. White's attack begins with Ne8+. If rook takes knight, decisive material is lost. Kg8 is forced because the rook on f8 would be otherwise lost. Nf6 follows, and the king must move to g7 to protect the rook. Again, rook takes f6 loses material. After Kg7 the first pregame is over. Now the decisive combination may begin. Q × f8+ K × f8, Re8+ Kg7, and Rg8 mate. Several diversion possibilities existed, but none of them was satisfactory from Black's point of view.

Another very common reason for diversion is double attack. A move is made to occupy either of two (or more) key squares. When the opponent parries one of the attacks he does not have time to parry the other. This is a different case from losing control over an important point, but the outcome is very similar when the focus of

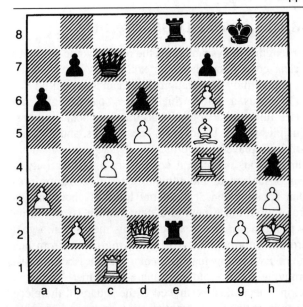

An example of double attack: White plays Re4. White queen threatens Q × g5+ and Qg7 mate. If Black exchanges by R × d2 the second threat, R × e8 mate, can be realized. No defence exists.

Figure 5.18 Double attack

attack changes. Figure 5.18 is a very simple example of double attack, which is a very powerful weapon in chess.

Diversion is a form of subgoaling. Diversion divides the task into two or more parts, in which one is carried out but the other is a necessary condition for the realization of the first. The subsidiary target squares, which the player attempts to occupy first, function as subgoals. This means that subgoals may also have a functional position in mental space, a subject we know literally nothing about at all.

Diversion and pregame are further examples of apperceptive processes in chess. There are undoubtedly many more. We know less about them than we know about the lowest conceptual level, which is move generation. However, there is every reason to believe that the nature of these processes would be similar to move generation.

SIMULATING THE SPATIAL LOGIC OF CHESS

After this rather lengthy analysis of cases the reader would probably like to gain a clear conception about the explanatory power of the semantic constraints of move generation. The main argument in this chapter is that chess is a game which has a spatial logic, and apperception uses this spatial logic in abstracting mental spaces. The lowest principles cannot be found in chess books, and they are not familiar to chess players; nevertheless all subjects use them. This kind of unconscious or implicit content-specific selectivity is an excellent demonstration of the complexity of information processes in human apperception. The spatial logic of chess has its origin in the rules of chess. Chess is a game which is played by moving pieces from one square to another. This means that a goal on a chessboard can only be achieved by moving pieces from one square to another. Everything that happens on a chessboard must take place by moving pieces from one square to another. To take a piece, the attacking piece must be moved to the square of the piece to be taken. To take back a piece, another piece must be moved to the square on which a piece was taken. The number of path, key, and target squares at which the balance of a position can be affected is always very small, and the number of pieces able to move to these squares even smaller. In fact, only one or two of the possible moves for each of the key pieces is needed. These 'screens' efficiently restrict the number of required operations.

The principles suggest that they could be studied by simulations. It should be possible to implement the principles in a computer program and see whether the mental spaces really would decrease in the way the theory claims. The computer simulation model M1 takes the position and the attacker's path as input and generates the related mental spaces (Saariluoma, in preparation). The program uses the principles of exchange, blockade and escape to abstract the mental space from the huge networks of moves. The crucial test for the program is the final size of the mental spaces.

Figure 5.19 presents two examples of mental space construction by M1. The spatial logic narrows the millions of paths down to human search space. Perhaps better than any argument these simulations show the explanatory power of spatial logic.

The combinations are not elementary, and M1 is very successful in producing the important mental spaces. The total number of moves it generates on the highest level is very small, which can

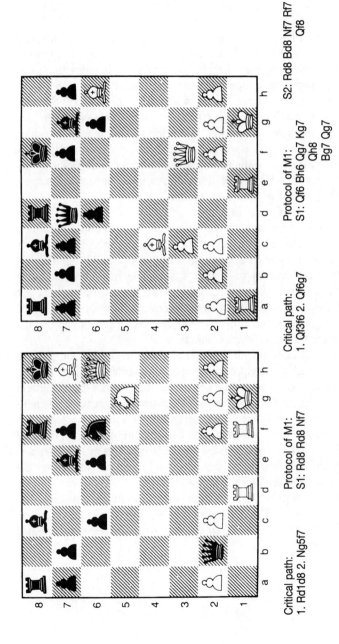

Critical path:
1. Rd1d8 2. Ng5f7

Protocol of M1:
S1: Rd8 Rd8 Nf7

Critical path:
1. Qf3f6 2. Qf6g7

Protocol of M1:
S1: Qf6 Bh6 Qg7 Kg7
                Qh8
                Bg7 Qg7

S2: Rd8 Bd8 Nf7 Rf7
                Qf8

Figure 5.19 Positions and mental spaces generated by a tentative simulation model M1 (coded by Harri Pöyhönen). The attacker's critical path is given and M1 constructs the search spaces using three move types: exchange, blockade and escape. (M1 does not provide capture signs in protocols)

be seen in the examples. Though the spaces are not absolutely human, they are clearly of human size. Since there are some twenty-five moves for each side, the basic problem spaces are something between three and four million alternatives.

In programming M1 we learned that human search is different from heuristic search in that it is dynamic. Human chess players use the sets of possible operators highly dynamically. In heuristic search models all imaginable operators are used in every depth of the search tree, and the best line is selected. This kind of operator generation is mechanical and static. It does not depend in any way on the problem. In contrast, the principles of search presented earlier enable human chess players to search dynamically. This means that they use only the operators that are necessary in the particular problem. If the problem or the problem subspace changes, so too does the set of operators used.

Dynamism is a very important property of human search. It explains why human search spaces are so small. People automatically sort out the relevant operators and apply only them. This is also a partial answer to a question which Dreyfus (1972) thought impossible: the control of search space. The mere possibility of simulating dynamic search shows that human search spaces are not restricted by any superhuman information processes, for the mind cleverly uses the properties of the task environment in the act of apperception to restrict search.

Perhaps the main teaching of M1 is that the pessimistic attitude people have had with respect to computers in analysing the content-specific processes is probably not as justified as has been thought (Dreyfus 1972, 1992). The semantic constraints can be implemented, and models can be used to demonstrate and to analyse complex cognitive processes, in which the discrimination of essential and inessential is central. Indeed, the analysis of chess players' apperception would be impossible without a tool like M1. No one has the stamina to study manually the jungles of moves to get a precise view of the systems of principles which apperception utilizes in constructing mental spaces. Thus M1 simulations show that the previous analysis really explains much of chess players' information integration in apperception.

APPERCEPTION AND SELECTIVE THINKING

Apperception is the core of content-specific selectivity in thinking. I think that we can be fairly certain of the justification for this classic concept and also of the fact that it is possible to study it using the concepts and methods of cognitive psychology. Indeed, it is a sign of the analytical power of this approach that it can turn this classic philosophical problem into an empirically analysable psychological concept.

It can be argued that in modern cognitive psychology the problem of mental representation formation has stimulated a number of theoretical concepts with strong intuitive assumptions. Examples of such concepts are stimulus equivalence, fixation, set, affordances, top-down v. bottom-up processing, pattern recognition, planning and schema theory (Anderson 1983, Duncker 1945, Gibson 1941, Maltzman 1955, Neisser 1976). So what is the use of postulating one new concept? These widely used notions are not unproblematic, and they lack expressibility. Their sheer number and vaguely defined borders show that sufficient generality has not been achieved. This means that research into representation formation is to some extent in a state of conceptual confusion. The suggested concepts do not provide suitable attributes with which to express all aspects of the mental representation construction that is so vital for modern cognitive psychology.

In the context of the research on chess players' thinking, three of the above notions have been relevant. They are planning, pattern recognition and schema activation (Chase and Simon 1973b, de Groot 1965, Newell and Simon 1972, Wilkins 1979). The intuitive problems with these concepts are typical, and they can be used to demonstrate the conceptual problems characteristic of the current psychology of thinking.

Planning, a term borrowed by Miller *et al.* (1960) from computer science, has had practically no applicability outside the problem-solving literature. Pattern recognition as the process of accessing familiar plans in long-term memory does not effectively apply to the study of genuine problem solving and the construction of new ideas (Chase and Simon 1973b, Duncker 1945, Holding 1985, Luchins 1942, Polya 1954, Saariluoma 1990b). Finally, schemata activation is an unclear notion because the notion of schemata does not express how our memory could produce concrete representations such as images (see also Alba and Hasher 1983, Neisser 1987). For example, a schematic memory could not play blindfold chess (Saariluoma 1991b). The notion of apperception is designed to emphasize the fact that the notion of object perception or any stimulus-bound notion, for example recognition, cannot express the process of constructing internal representations in thinking. The cognitive constraints and content-specific processes are absolutely essential. The selectivity in apperception is content specific. Yet apperception is an umbrella concept for the very large number of known and unknown processes ensuring that our representations will have senseful contents.

The use of the term apperception is not an absolute necessity. No theoretical term is absolutely necessary, but cognitive psychologists should not underestimate the importance of the intuitive and imaginary contents of theoretical concepts (Nagel 1961). Behaviourism should be a sufficient warning concerning the discouraging consequences of minimally expressive theoretical concepts. Ramsey elimination-type processes in which all theoretical terms are reduced into an observational language are misplaced, because they do not open new research possibilities (Tuomela 1977). Pure observation language does not suggest anything, because all the observations have the same degree of relevance. In terms of observation language the number of stones on the beach is equivalent to the number of particles in an atom. This is why we should try to build as expressive and discriminative theoretical languages as possible.

Because recent research into chess players' problem solving has now made it possible to discuss the notion of apperception directly, this opportunity should be used (Saariluoma 1990b, 1991b, 1992b). The first empirical 'attacks' have provided us with some important knowledge about the process. First, it has been possible to show that the human mind is able to use very simple principles to select among the relevant and irrelevant information. Out of millions of possible paths people are able to select just a few.

The cognitive constraints are very elementary, but they seem to operate unconsciously. People never mention them in protocols, though they obviously follow them. One cannot find them in chess books, and I have found that chess players are not familiar with them. The cognitive constraints seem to be very much like the grammatical rules. We follow them unconsciously and unintentionally to represent the environment in a senseful manner.

Chess players learn the basic structure of the environment very early. They use a large number of unconscious principles in constructing representations. These plans and other chess concepts may be knit into the same representation, so that it has its self-consistent structure. Apperception is important for our understanding of selective thinking. It enables people to select on the basis of content. Capacity-based selectivity, which was considered in the two previous chapters, cannot thus be the only form of selectivity utilized by mind. Now we know that capacity is not enough to explain all selective information processing. People use contents, and the purpose of apperception research is to show how this is possible. To find the laws, principles and preconditions of content-specific selectivity is a decisive problem in all research into human apperception.

Chapter 6

Restructuring and subjective search spaces

In this chapter I will consider protocols as wholes: that is, as subjective search spaces. Mental spaces are constructed by apperception. They are self-consistent, senseful and articulated wholes. Each element in a mental space makes sense and has a reason for its being an element in the particular mental space. No comparable consistency can be found in the contents of subjective search spaces. While mental spaces are senseful and self-consistent, subjective search spaces are just mixtures of content-specific, but mostly unrelated, mental spaces (Newell and Simon 1972).

The moves in different mental spaces of one and the same subjective search space need not bear any relation to one another. Two different mental spaces may be in opposition to each other. This means that the same semantic elements are used in each for different purposes. It is perfectly possible, for example, for the same pieces to be moved into different squares, or for different pieces to be imagined in one and the same square in different mental spaces. This means that the mental spaces are absolutely incompatible and they cannot be represented simultaneously.

Mental space construction is an apperceptive process, but processing subjective search spaces requires a new cognitive process. That process is restructuring. Mental spaces are apperceived but the shifts between different mental spaces are no longer an apperceptive process; they comprise restructuring. By restructuring I mean a mental process that changes one mental space into another. Restructuring is a classic Gestalt term (Duncker 1945, Wertheimer 1945). By restructuring, the Gestaltists normally referred to changes in the perceptual field; that is, in the way people perceived the objects (e.g. Ohlsson 1992). Though in the first enthusiasm of cognitive psychology restructuring was forgotten, it has recently aroused interest among researchers (Kaplan and Simon 1990, Ohlsson 1984a, b, 1992).

Nevertheless, the classic interpretation of restructuring has only limited use here, because in this work the main interest lies in the semantic contents of representations and not in their perceptual effects. In particular, the distinction between perception and apperception makes it necessary to elucidate the concept of restructuring. My main point is that it is much more the content of the representation than the perceptual field which is important. The content of the representation, even in such a basically visual environment as chess, is independent of the stimulus that is actually perceived. Hence, the classic Gestalt interpretations of restructuring in problem solving are useful but narrow in scope and this makes it essential to turn from perceptual to representational concepts.

Restructuring is characterized by a change in representation and this may sometimes also have perceptual consequences. None the less, the essence of restructuring is at a representational level and not a new way of perceiving the environment. It is the contents of representations which are restructured in the first place and the perceptual effects are just consequences for the changes at a representational level. Indeed, no perceived stimuli are needed in restructuring.

In practice, this means that we must pay attention not only to stages in restructuring but also to its internal logic. The stages or types of restructuring, such as insight or incubation, do not tell us much about what happens at a representational level. Why is a representation restructured? How do we know that a representation is insufficient, and indeed do we always know that we are unable effectively to represent the reality? To answer these kinds of questions it is necessary to interpret the contents of the concept of restructuring more widely than did the Gestaltists, and also to pay attention to its content-specific dynamics. Fortunately, this wider interpretation can be made in the context of subjective search spaces.

THE ORGANIZATION OF SUBJECTIVE SEARCH SPACES

A subjective search space contains all the moves generated by a subject when trying to find a move in a position, and I have already argued that it is a collection of incompatible mental spaces. In protocols subjective search spaces consist of episodes, which are move sequences from the initial position to some goal position.

The main issue of interest to researchers is the macro-organization of subjective search spaces: that is, the flow of episodes and mental spaces through protocols (de Groot 1965, Newell and Simon 1972). A most important observation was made by de Groot (1965) on this topic. He noticed that the expansions of the subjective search space are not systematic. The best characterization of the development of subjective search spaces is 'progressive deepening'. By progressive deepening de Groot meant that players often return to the previously searched mental spaces to improve them, though they would have been concentrating on other mental spaces in the interim.

De Groot saw the generation of a subjective search space as development of a problem itself. In this he follows Duncker (1945) and Selz (1913). The idea of a solution in the successive phases of deepening finds a new and improved formulation. It becomes more concrete, and the key points in the solution are formed. In fact one could also see problem development as the development of different simultaneous subproblems and the development of a total goal conception.

Unfortunately, we do not know much more about the logical and content-specific mechanisms behind episodic and mental space shifts. Selz (1913), the Gestaltists and de Groot (1965) concentrated mostly on the analysis of the phases of the problem-solving process and gave relatively little weight to the contents of the thought and the logic that controls the changes in the contents. Thus, chess protocols must be reanalysed in order to learn more about the mechanisms of mental space shifts, and this work must begin with the logic of restructuring. The logic of hypothesis testing and the task-necessary decisions make for the most general contents in chess players' thinking, and consequently this is the most general 'layer' in chess players' thinking. When we understand this level, the more specific information structures can be discussed.

THE LOGIC OF HYPOTHESIS TESTING

Most psychologists have known that subjects feel the need to convince themselves about the truthfulness of their own thoughts (Newell and Simon 1972). Before the final action is carried out, it is necessary to eliminate errors by simulating the reality and thus testing out ideas. It is better simply to think first and contemplate the consequences of alternative courses of action carefully, before the actual measures are enacted. This cautiousness may sometimes greatly reduce the consequences and costs of errors. This is why the logic of generating and testing hypotheses is important in all theories of human thinking.

De Groot (1965) and Newell and Simon (1972) use the term 'verification tree' to express the idea of proving the truthfulness of a solution. To Dewey (1910), the proof of a hypothesis was one essential stage in the thought process. The necessity of proof is evident also in all models of correct scientific thinking from the Milesian philosophers onwards. Equally the ideas of verification and falsification are the key concepts in Popper's (1959) models of scientific thinking. The position in human thinking of generating and testing hypotheses is so obvious that any serious theory of thinking must entail the concept of hypothesis verification. This conception concerns how people convince themselves of the truthfulness of their thoughts.

The ultimate goal of mental space abstraction is to find a solution to a problem. Chess players' thinking is not just move searching and choosing. They must also find moves that are so good that they cannot be refuted. This means that the opponent must not have any move which would prevent the player from achieving the goal position. It also means that none of the opponents' moves must lead to a poorer outcome than the goal position. In practice this means that the opponent must not have a move available that has the consequence of forcing the player to an unadvantageous diversion.

Mental spaces are hypothetical solutions in the human mind, and they must be verified before they can be accepted. This means that the player must be certain that no refutation exists. If there is one, the goal is not reachable. When the move has been executed, no return is possible. In this respect, chess players' thinking is very similar to the thinking of any professional. An engineer, for example, who has constructed a faulty structure must face the possibility of failure after the structure has been completed. This is why pretesting is so important in engineering.

Generate a hypothesis ⟵⟶ Test it

Figure 6.1 Problem-solving cycle

The alternation of hypothesis generation and verification is one of the basic structures in human thinking, and can be found in the work of Dewey (1910), de Groot (1965), Polya (1954), or in Newell and Simon's (1972) theories of human problem solving. It can be called the problem-solving cycle. The problem-solving cycle is the alternation between two modes of thinking: hypothesis generation and hypothesis testing (see Figure 6.1). Without the alternation of these two modes, human thinking would simply comprise blind reactions to stimulus situations.

The basic logic behind hypothesis testing is simple. If the hypothesis can be verified, the corresponding action, i.e. the move, is accepted. If no verification can be found, a new idea must be sought and verified. This means also that a player must restructure, unless for psychological or some other reasons he or she wants to gamble, but this is a rare occasion in chess. Restructuring is simply the only way to refocus thinking from an unrealizable and impossible mental space to one that is possibly realizable.

CLOSING A MENTAL SPACE

To verify a mental space, a player must know that the opponent cannot find, in any branch of the subtree, a terminal position which is more advantageous for the opponent than the main goal position. The game theoretical minimax logic entails that the opponent always makes a move which minimizes the players' chances, and thus if a hole in the move network can be found, a rational and capable opponent tries to utilize this opportunity to maximize his or her own expectations (Newell and Simon 1972, Simon 1974b, c).

The act of proving the goal position as the maximal expectation for the opponent can be called closing, because it attempts to show that in all branches of the subtree, no refutation can be found. A mental space which necessarily leads to the main goal position can be called a closed mental space. A space in which the opponent can avoid the main goal and achieve a relatively good terminal position can be called open mental space.

The core of a mental space is the critical path: that is, a sequence of moves from an initial situation to some target square and goal position. The task of verification in the first place is to show that this path is closed. Since closing a path means that the opponent has no means to prevent the active side from achieving the goal and that only the opponent's moves which end in the path can prevent the

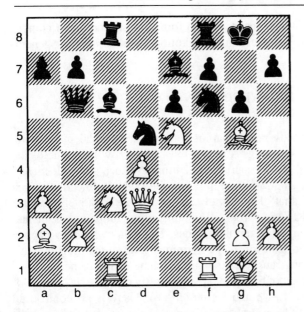

N × d5, B × d5; is that possible? d7 is free then. B × d5, B × f6 B × f6, Nd7 Qd8 can be done . . . N × d5 N × d5, B × d5 B × g5 – no nothing then

Figure 6.2 Goal shifting within a mental space in the protocol of Max Euwe. Here the originally promising line is refuted in the lower episode by taking with knight to d5 instead of bishop. The space cannot thus be closed
Note: Translation into abbreviated algebraic system by P.S.
Source: de Groot (1965, p. 411)

player from achieving the goal, the core of closing is the spanning of mental space. The player must find all the opponent's moves which may end up in the path and eliminate them.

To close a mental space is to ensure that the opponent has no effective moves coming on to the path or no effective counter-actions to the player's own. Here the term effective refers to the fact that the goal position must be abandoned for a more adverse terminal position. Consequently, the main goal is not reachable and the goal of the mental space must be shifted. Figure 6.2 provides us with an example of goal shifting within a mental space.

The final form of a mental space thus can be accounted for after the player has found all the relevant moves and hence is able to determine the real goal position. This knowledge is needed in evaluation of mental spaces, which forms the second major component of mental space closing in addition to move network generation.

STRATEGIC KNOWLEDGE IN CLOSING MENTAL SPACES

The network of all moves that are relevant in a mental space is not sufficient for its closing. A player must also know the value of the terminal nodes. No one can generate infinitely deep and wide mental spaces. On the contrary, research into the size of subjective search spaces shows that their depth and width are relatively modest (Charness 1981b, de Groot 1965). The tree comprising a mental space has a number of terminal nodes. To predict what may happen beyond the horizon of these terminal modes the player must evaluate the long-range or strategic outcome of the game.

Evaluation cannot be based on very swiftly changing properties of chess positions (Euwe and Kramer 1956). There is no point in an evaluation based on transient factors, because evaluation must predict the future course of a game. The best result can be achieved when the attribute on which evaluation is based must persist on the board for a long time. These kinds of permanent properties in chess theory are called chess strategic properties or chess strategic rules.

Typically, strategic properties concern the structure of pawn chains, the type and number of pieces on the board, permanently weak squares, etc. Material – that is, the number and the strengths of the pieces on the board – is a typical strategic property. The difficulty of strategic evaluation is caused by different types of compensations. For example, one may lose a piece, but gain a very strong position as a result. This means that one strategic property must be evaluated against another which is of a very different type. No concrete moves are usually necessary in strategic thinking. Exceptions are manoeuvres that aim to place a piece on a strong square. Even then the precise order of moves is largely irrelevant. These kinds of dynamic properties of chess positions are very difficult to evaluate precisely (de Groot 1965).

Perhaps two practical examples might show the problems which top-level chess players have in evaluating chess positions. They are from the games of Fischer and Tal respectively. These examples are far too complicated to be calculated through to the very end or to be closed by any simple evaluative schemata. Players must have

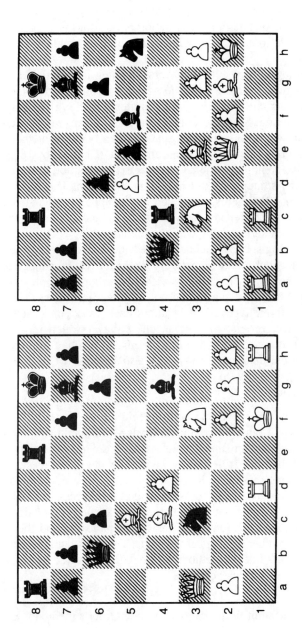

Figure 6.3 Two very difficult positions: Byrne–Fischer (1956), Botvinnik–Tal (1960). In the first, Black plays Be6 and in the second Nf4

confidence in their positional assessment. If they have overlooked something, the lost material makes winning the game a trivial task for the opponent. The genius-like quality of players like Tal and Fischer lies in the fact that their evaluation of positions is so precise that they are able to emerge as winners despite the complexities of the combinations.

Lay psychology divides chess players' thinking into tactical and strategic. Tactical thinking is short-range planning in which immediate threats are important, while strategic thinking concerns long-range planning. Strategic thinking in chess means very much the same as in war or business life: that is, to unify different short-term tactical goals under one long-term goal (Clausewitz 1832/1978). It is also commonly argued that there is no position in which both tactics and strategy are not important. Since this lay psychological difference between strategy and tactics appears in hundreds of chess books, the difference between strategic and tactical thinking must be taken seriously by chess psychologists.

Some psychologists have acknowledged the difference between strategic and tactical thinking, but very little concrete research has been carried out so far. De Groot's (1965) data on chess players' thinking show that chess players do not only register moves. They pick up very different types of information: lines, weak points, static and dynamic factors, etc. In general, chess players often rely on rather ill-defined concepts, which may be highly intuitive and very difficult to model computationally (see also Dreyfus 1972, 1992, Dreyfus and Dreyfus 1986).

De Groot writes:

> In spite of the extensive body of strategic theory, there exists a large number of typical strategic methods – rules and exceptions to them – that have remained nameless. They are not registered in 'official' theory but still form a weapon in the chess master's arsenal. Among these are all sorts of manoeuvres, offensive and defensive buildups, ways of regrouping the pieces etc. The general methods of piece co-operation appear to be particularly difficult to describe in detail, to treat systematically, and therefore to pass to other students of the game. Thus the state of affairs with regard to strategic methods differs only in degree from the tactical methods discussed above . . .
>
> (de Groot 1965, pp. 303–304)

The important point in the paragraph is de Groot's methodological conception of chess strategy. Like some chess masters such as Lasker (1947), he sees only a difference in degree between strategy and tactics. This means that according to de Groot, strategic properties of chess positions may suggest moves to players.

Newell and Simon (1972) followed de Groot, but in heuristic search models they gave strategic rules a much less active role than he did. Strategic rules were used to prune the game tree and not so much to suggest new ideas. Newell and Simon (1972) also noticed that chess players generally use few if any strategic rules in evaluating positions. Human chess players did not act like machines by simply adding the values of the parameters. They somehow selected the relevant rules from the irrelevant (Saariluoma 1984).

Charness (1977) suggested an idea that undoubtedly brings an important new issue into the discussion. He argued that chess players try to achieve certain position types. For example, they could exchange pieces to achieve a pawn ending with one pawn more than the opponent, because they know that they will then be able to win the game. To Holding (1985), evaluation is a major process. It is the second main component of his SEEK theory of chess players' problem solving. Masters are better than novices because they can evaluate chess positions better. In fact, chess skill is predicted better by evaluation than recall (Holding 1985, 1992a, b, Holding and Reynolds 1985). Saariluoma's (1984) experiment showed that experts were clearly superior to less experienced players in strategic evaluation, and these results support Holding's (1985) point of view.

Obviously, strategy is an exceptionally important part of chess thinking, and the difference between strategic and tactical thinking must be made clear conceptually and functionally. The crucial problem is: how are strategic and tactical thinking intertwined in chess players' thought processes? How do strategic concepts aid tactical thinking? Only in this way can we understand how strategic evaluation affects the restructuring of mental spaces.

It is very characteristic of strategic thinking that evaluation takes place in the terminal nodes of mental spaces. Subjects generate move series and then they evaluate the terminal positions (Saariluoma and Hohlfeld 1994). It is also common to find a number of evaluative sentences at the beginning of a new episode. In contrast, intermediate evaluative and strategic sentences are seldom found (Saariluoma 1990b, Saariluoma and Hohlfeld 1994).

This suggests that evaluation concerns an episode together with

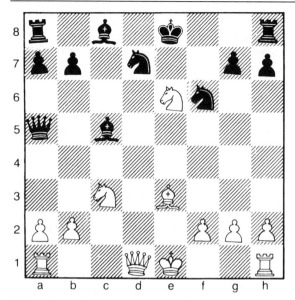

1) B × c5 and Black should take with knight to c5. Then I could play Qd6 and threat Nc7 but that is rubbish . . . 2) I could build some pressure, but there is no forcing continuation. 3) As said, the position looks like an attacking position. 4) But that all is meaningless. 5) I had a long-lasting option in d5. 6) Also the space advantage and then – perhaps White could before long occupy e5.

Figure 6.4 Examples of evaluation

its corresponding mental space as a whole, and that evaluation provides targets for search. Heuristic search would naturally suggest that the major part of evaluative sentences could be found in each depth of a game tree. This means that the major function of evaluation is not tree pruning at all, but target setting.

In Figure 6.4, the function of evaluation is really to pose a target and assess the value of a closed episode. The protocol provides no support for heuristic search type thinking. Chess-playing computer programs at the moment work fundamentally differently from human problem solvers with respect to evaluation.

It is the spatial logic of mental spaces which enables human chess players to use the terminal node evaluation. It is sufficient to know the target square and to span a mental space. Spatial logic controls the rest of move generation, and no intermediate evaluation is needed. Only the terminal nodes must be evaluated in closing a mental space.

The target is a strategic element rather than a tactical unit. Mate, for example, is a strategic goal in chess. In fact it is the ultimate strategic goal. Material advantage is also a strategic factor as well as resulting in the occupation of a weak square. It is the task of strategic thinking to define which targets are important. Therefore, evaluation is needed in the beginning as well as at the end of episodes, but intermediate evaluation is of lesser importance (Saariluoma and Hohlfeld 1994).

Thus mental space closing has two components. First, subjects must be able to generate all the relevant moves of a mental space and thereafter they must be able to evaluate the terminal nodes correctly. If they manage in these two tasks, they know precisely the value of the mental space. Of course, this is not always an easy task and errors are common.

CLOSING AND RESTRUCTURING

Closing and restructuring are linked in an important way. If a player fails to close a space, or if its goal is not sufficiently important, he or she must restructure the mental space. It is pointless to try to follow through an inadequate idea, and therefore restructuring is required in order to find something better. Of course, the ultimate reason for the failure in closing may be in the generation of moves or in evaluation. The reasons may also be right or wrong (see Figure 6.5), but the effect of negative closing is always the same. The concept of closing is thus the very key to the control of restructuring and the generation of subjective search spaces in chess.

Chess players abandon mental spaces because they are not able to close them (see Figure 6.6). They are unable to show that the opponent could be forced to the planned goal position. Consequently, they must improve old mental spaces or find new ideas. If they fail in closing, they must restructure and shift their attention from one space to another in order to search for a solution.

The example in Figure 6.6 shows that the subject is not satisfied with the correct mental space because he is unable to close it properly. Similar consequences can be found when a terminal position is felt to be undesirable. Figure 6.6 provides an example. If a mental space can be closed, evaluation is the decisive reason for the acceptance or refutation of a mental space. In Figure 6.8 (p. 151) the subject doubts the value of f6, then he finds the refutation and restructures effectively.

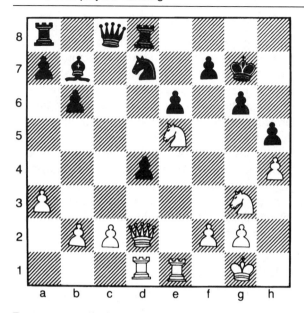

From a protocol of a master:
N × h5+ g × h5, Qg5+ Kf8, Qh6+ Ke8, Qh8+ Ke7, Ng6+ f × g6, Qg7+
Ke8 and mate; no, he can play Kd6 then Kc6 . . . this is difficult . . . Rd4
at least . . . Rd4 Bd5, can I find anything? . . . I have soon used all ten
minutes . . . (*experimenter*: yes) I should make a move (*experimenter*:
yes) . . . Oh . . . A moment; Qg5 first . . . that might be the most sensible
alternative . . .that will be followed by N × h5+, king escapes; I have to
look first . . . N × h5+ g × h5, Qg5 and Ne5, well he can play loose
moves . . . f6 opens . . . if Black exchanges on e5 surely Qg5 would be a
reasonable move . . . that was a fast look . . .
(In this fragment the master is not able to close the mental space after
the right move N × h5 and restructures by playing the queen first to g5.
The move is not a particularly good one, because N × e5 gives a big
advantage for Black after either Q × e5 Kg8 or N × h5+ Kf8.)

Figure 6.5 Erroneous restructuring

The decisive insight in considering chess players' restructuring is
that the control of mental space alternation begins with internal
control. Mental spaces can be accepted if no refutation can be
found. If a refutation can be found, an alternative mental space
also must be found. The only exception is deliberate bluffing,
which is used to unsettle the opponent or if the player is running
out of time, but in practice it is a rarity. In this way restructuring is
caused by a failure to close a mental space.

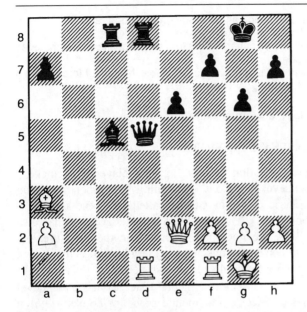

Perhaps B × f2+. Looks very promising. The rook cannot take back. If queen takes, d1, then Q takes f7 . . . then Kh8 Bb2+, yes, Black loses. Well, to take on f2 is impossible . . . so if there is nothing else . . .

I have to recalculate B × f2 [. . .] yes, this looks difficult . . . Is this a lasting advantage? Black has an extra pawn. No clear continuation to be seen . . .

Aha! Let's take with queen to d1. Rook takes back, rook takes, the queen has to take, bishop takes a3 and rook threatens to win the queen by moving to c1 . . . and if queen moves it will be a back-row mate . . . this seems to be foolproof . . . White has no intermediate moves . . . and king no escape. Yes, Black wins a piece.

Figure 6.6 Evaluation and restructuring

Figure 6.7 provides a schematic presentation of the logic of mental spaces, of refutation and of restructuring.

Considerations on the internal control of restructuring may be concluded with these examples, the next section being devoted to the analysis of some control mechanisms that work outside individual mental spaces. Attention will be paid especially to the decision mechanisms that control the allocation of resources.

(1) If I can close this space and the outcome is good, accept.
(2) If I cannot close a space, restructure.
(3) If no opponent move can force me to a worse position than the goal, the space is closed.
(4) If the opponent has no path moves available, he cannot force me to a worse position than the goal position.

Figure 6.7 The logic of restructuring

TASK-NECESSARY DECISIONS

During the move selection process, a chess player must make a number of metalevel decisions concerning the problem-solving process itself. These decisions can be called task-necessary decisions (Saariluoma 1984). They are often automatized, but may also be conscious. They are not much discussed in the literature, but some preliminary considerations are necessary here. It is the task of later research to go into the details of task-necessary decisions.

If a chess player fails to close a mental space, he has a metalevel problem. He has to select a new mental space, or he has to go on with the current space and try to find something new. The next example (Figure 6.8) demonstrates this point. In the protocol, the subject cannot find the queen sacrifice, and therefore he starts to defend the f2 pawn, which seems to be vulnerable. To change the focus of his attention, he has to make a task-necessary decision. He must decide whether to continue the search within the active mental space or to restructure.

Obviously, the decision to restructure mental space cannot be avoided. Even the avoidance of mental space shifting is a decision, and this is why task-necessary decisions are unavoidable. They are essential for the smooth course of thinking, and they also bear on the theory of cognitive errors.

The mental space shifting decision is often automatic, because subjects do not pay any conscious attention to it. How often this decision is automatic we do not know, but it may also be conscious. In the above protocol (Figure 6.8), for example, the belief in the black queen's defensive power after Qf8 is so strong that a new goal comes to the fore: the defence of the white f2 pawn. The change is quite explicit, because the subject expresses it verbally.

These partially controlled and partially automatic restructuring decisions are highly interesting, but unfortunately they belong to almost totally unresearched areas of chess psychology. At the

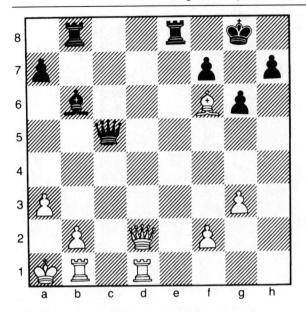

Qh6 comes to my mind. Threatens mate in g7. Black defends himself by
Qf8 . . . and it is sufficient . . . There is no clear move in this position . . . I
pay attention to the f2 pawn . . . The other possible move is Qh6, but it
does not give anything. Bishop does not play any role on f6. One way to
parry the pressure against f2 would be Bd4 . . . I would end up Bd4.

Figure 6.8 Unsatisfactory closing (Black to move)

moment not much more can be done but to point to the existence
of the problem.

Another important task-necessary decision is the termination decision (Figure 6.9). By this I mean the decision about the termination of the problem-solving process. The decision concerns whether
the solver wants to go on, or to stop the problem-solving process and
make the final choice.

The termination decision is very much like the mental space shift
decision. It may be almost automatic, but under some conditions it
may also be conscious. When it is automatic and when it is
conscious is not known as yet. These two task-necessary decision
types are important in restructuring because abandoning search is
one of the major elements in fixation, and the two decisions deserve
much more research.

A mental space shifting decision can also have a strong influence

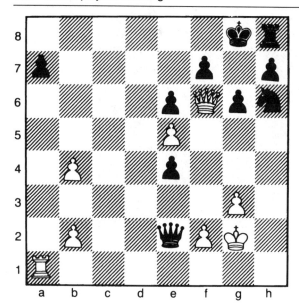

[. . .] I still calculate R × a7 Qf3+, Kg1 Qd1+ should be the best . . . after that king may go to h2. No it cannot because Ng4+, king somewhere and knight takes f6. e × f6 and h6 or h5. [. . .] Would there be any alternative move order? Not really . . . h5 always . . . Yes, I would play Qd8+, which is a draw.

(Here, despite explicit reference to alternative move order the subject overlooks the move Rc1, which parries the perpetual check and threatens back-row mate. Consequently, White wins.)

Figure 6.9 Termination decision

on a further course of the solving process. If a subject fails to close a correct mental space and begins to restructure by moving to another problem space, he may be lost for good. When a subject searches for a solution in the wrong mental space, it seems to be very difficult to find the right one. The mechanisms of apperception simply blockade the information that would be needed to build an alternative, correct mental space.

There is very little more that can be said about task-necessary decisions. More empirical research is needed. One thing is evident, however: task-necessary decisions are central in restructuring and form a part of metalevel control. Task-necessary decisions must be made explicitly or implicitly, consciously or unconsciously. So task-necessary decisions are always a part of the structure of the problem solving process.

The analysis of the cognitive structures behind mental space shifts in subjective search spaces can be closed now. The picture is idealized, because mostly it discusses the generation of subjective search space when things go well. However, error is the soul of chess, and thus in the following sections the nature of cognitive errors and failures must be discussed.

FIXATION OF MENTAL SPACES

Mental spaces are subspaces and thus abstractions of the basic problem space. That is, a very large number of alternative paths are screened out or neglected, and the search concentrates only on those that are most essential. This does not mean that the alternatives which chess players find consist of all possible relevant paths, and thus an important question arises: what is the relationship between the active mental spaces and the mental spaces which are unconscious, implicit, or yet to be discovered?

When people apperceive one mental space they cannot attend to the alternatives. The capacity of their attention does not allow the simultaneous representing and manipulating of multiple mental spaces. This might lead to a blockade in which the processing of one mental space interferes with and impairs the processing of alternative mental spaces. Indeed, this is very much the classic problem of fixation, but on a representational level. If the alternative mental spaces really interfere with each other, this would mean that apperception is related to fixation, set, and other similar phenomena (Duncker 1945, Wertheimer 1945).

Saariluoma (1990b) tried to find answers to these questions by presenting a number of experienced amateur chess players with the position in Figure 6.10. The position is deceptively simple and seems to be a case of a very simple mating theme called smothered mate. Apparently, White should play the variation 1. Qe6+ Kh8, 2. Nf7+ Kg8, 3. Nh6++ Kh8, 4. Qg8+ R × g8, 5. Nf7 mate. This continuation, which was selected very swiftly by all experienced players, is not optimal. There is a better line hidden in the position. White could also play 1. Qe6+ Kh8, 2. Nf7+ Kg8, 3. N × d8+! Kh8, 4. Qe8, and mate is reached one move sooner.

Why did none of the nine strong chess players select this continuation in the experiment by Saariluoma (1990b)? The answer is quite simple. They did not notice or apperceive it. When the experimenter began to give cues to the subjects to lead them to the correct solution, they had great difficulty in finding it, as was demonstrated in the protocol example. All the experienced subjects first tried some other line, and only after prolonged cuing could they find the shortest way to achieve checkmate (Saariluoma 1990b, 1992).

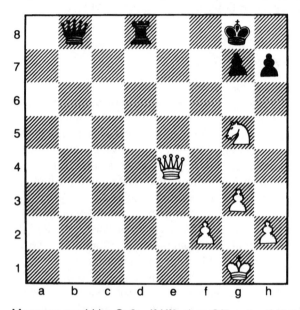

My move would be Qe6+. If Kf8, then Qf7 mate. If Kh8 then Nf7+ Kg8, Nh6++. If then Kf8, Qf7 mate and Kh8, Qg8+ R × g8. The rook move is obligatory, because the king cannot move, and then Nf7 mate. (*Experimenter*: This was fine, but I must ask, if there is a faster mate or better move?) No! (*Experimenter*: Are you sure?) Well, Q × h7+ Kf8 and Qh8+ Ke7, Q × h7 and Kd8, but the king can escape. The previous continuation is the best. (*Experimenter*: Is there something else you can play?) Yes, you can play Qc4 and achieve the same result as in the first case except that the rook can delay mate one move by opposing on d5. (*Experimenter*: Something which makes your game shorter. Is there still something more efficient?) No. (*Experimenter*: OK, let's look together at the main line: Qe6+ Kh8, Nf7+ Kg8. What did you move here?) Nh6++. (*Experimenter*: Do you have any alternatives?) Yes, you can take rook with the knight, but that . . . that would . . . let's see. I am not sure . . . Oh! *If* you take the rook, the king has to go. If king f8, Qf7 mate, and if it goes to h8 then queen mate e8.

Figure 6.10 A position and protocol with a suboptimal solution and strong fixation

Smothered mate is a very familiar theme of a combination, and finding it is an easy problem for experienced chess players. All the skilled subjects knew the position and could name it. Smothered mate is, in fact, a typical spatio-temporal chunk which has been discussed elsewhere (Fine 1965). In problem-solving language it could be called a plan, but this term must not then be confused with the chess term 'plan', which refers to the strategic conduct of a game. Plans are in a psychological sense a learned sequence of actions (e.g. Miller *et al.* 1960). They are conceptual structures which can be used and are used to categorize the environment.

In chess, the actions are moves, and plans are pre-learned methods of playing (de Groot 1965). They are normally a learned series of moves which are associated with some characteristic properties of positions. The properties may be piece patterns or strategic features such as an open line or a pair of bishops (Chase and Simon 1973b, Newell and Simon 1972). However, plans are not mental spaces, because plans are information structures in long-term memory, and in genuine problem solving they can very easily be used as such without modifications. They form one part of the conceptual knowledge used in the abstraction of mental spaces, but they are not mental spaces. Mental spaces are active representations. Plans in long-term memory could be called prototypical problem spaces, because they are just sketches of mental spaces.

The recognition of a familiar plan or prototypical problem space, such as smothered mate, leads to the formation of a mental space. The formation of the mental spaces is in this case based on a familiar and very commonly encountered plan (Chase and Simon 1973b, de Groot 1965, Saariluoma 1990). The recognition process activates a prototypical problem space in a chess player's long-term memory and apperception assimilates it with relevant additional information such as the precise locations of moves, etc.

The actual solution did not appear to players through an instant recognition process. On the contrary, they needed very marked cues before being able to construct the final solution. The differences between the first mental space and the final solution are obvious. In the latter case subsequent cuing and thus a great deal of extra information is needed for finding the solution, for no familiar model could be used. Consequently, the mental space formation process in the first case can be seen as simple recognition but in the latter case this is impossible.

FIXATION IN THE ENDGAME

Fixation and mental space abstraction are not characteristic only of middle game combinations. Fixation phenomena can also be found in endgames. An example is provided by an experiment with a famous Reti endgame (Fine 1964). In Figure 6.11, an ending by Reti is presented with colours reversed (Fine 1964). However, this is not the famous Reti ending, in which White is able to achieve a draw with a most unlikely king's manoeuvre. The position is a variant of the famous ending. This ending can be won by Black, because Black's king is on a7 and not on a6 as in the famous Reti endgame, a factor that permits Black to blockade the passed pawn by the manoeuvre Kb8–c8.

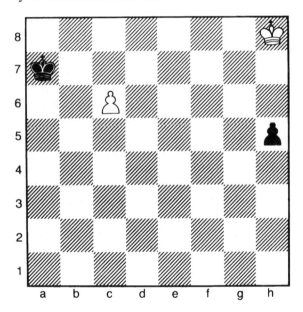

Master: If 1. king g7 h4, 2. Kf6 h3, 3. Ke7 h2, 4. Kd7 h1Q, 5. c7 draw. From the beginning 1. Kg7 h4, 2. Kf6 Kb6, Black wins. 1. Kg7, h4, 2. Kf6, Kb6, 3. Ke5. If now 3. –, h3 then 4. Kd6. If 3.–, K × c6 then 4. Kf4 and draw! If Kb6 then Ke5 and threatens Kd6. If c plays . . . king takes c7, 6, so king f4 draws. That's all. My move? Kg7. (The master overlooks the move Kb8 instead of Kb6. This move is not possible in the original Reti's task. Knowing Reti's endgame well, he is fixated by it and does not pay attention to the best moves.)

Figure 6.11 Endgame with fixation

The master in his protocol thinks that the ending is the famous Reti ending and overlooks the blockade variation. He is obviously fixated by the familiar plan, as were the subjects in the smothered mate experiment. Since four of the seven subjects confused this position with Reti's famous ending, this is a very clear indication of mental space fixation in endgames (Saariluoma 1992b). Familiar plans fixate the chess players.

Mental spaces are problem subspaces and the experiments show that there is a strong connection between apperception or mental subspace abstraction and, on the other hand, fixation- and set-type classic phenomena. Hence, improved psychological knowledge about the abstraction of mental spaces should improve our under-standing of fixation-, set- and einstellung-like phenomena (Duncker 1945, Gibson 1941, Wertheimer 1945). Mental spaces should also clarify how our conceptual representations control the other cogni-tive functions, perception, imagery and memory and they are perhaps crucial in fixation and other similar mental phenomena.

FURTHER EXPERIMENTS ON MENTAL SPACE FIXATION

In the middle game experiment of Figure 6.10, the skilled subjects first saw the smothered mate and only afterwards did they apply the second plan beginning with Q × h7. It would appear that the smothered mate plan had somehow blocked or prevented experts from immediately seeing this alternative. This means that subjects may actually overlook the alternative solutions, because they are satisfied with the one they are able to find.

Saariluoma (1990b) carried out one experiment to study the effects of the familiar mental spaces on apperceiving the less familiar. Two groups of subjects were shown almost similar chess positions. In the positions shown to the first group, there were two solutions, one familiar and the other unfamiliar. The positions shown to the second group contained only the unfamiliar continua-tion. It was assumed that if active mental spaces prevent subjects from noticing the alternatives, the unfamiliar continuation would commonly be found in the second group. Consequently, it could be argued that the first group did not see the second line because the familiar continuation prevented them from doing so. The hypothesis proved to be correct, since there were approximately 60 per cent more successful solutions following the unfamiliar continuations in the second group than in the first (Figure 6.12).

Plans or prototypical problem spaces, i.e. pre-learned mental spaces in LTM, act like conceptual structures. This seems paradoxical, because they mostly do not even have a name. But the idea that they are conceptual structures is justified, because these prototypical problem spaces are used to categorize the environment. They are prelinguistic concepts: that is, conceptual structures without specific names. These kinds of conceptual structure seem to play a much larger role in chess than we had previously thought. They control our perception and segmentation of the physical environment.

The selectivity of planning must not be underestimated. The phenomenon shows that standard planning language is not sufficient to express all aspects of the construction of problem representations. The recognized plan is used to abstract the relevant aspects of a problem situation in abstract mental spaces, but it does not involve mental space itself. Further, if the active mental space is not the right one, it interferes with the abstraction of alternatives. Chess players cannot study more than one mental space at a time, because the limited capacity of the human attentional system prevents them from processing several mental spaces in parallel. Therefore, an analysis of the perceptual processes in

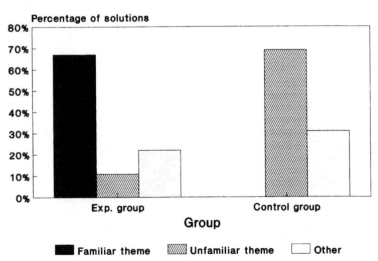

Figure 6.12 Fixation by a familiar theme

activating and adapting plans is essential for any theoretical attempt to understand human chess players' problem solving.

It seems that fixation is a metalevel error. People are contented with the continuation they have found, and therefore they do not actively pursue a new solution, even though this would be reachable. Another problem is that the alternative solutions may be very difficult to find, and this presumably increases the strength of fixation.

INSIGHT AND RESTRUCTURING

In classic Gestalt theory, insight was a highly valued form of restructuring. Clearly, insight is an impressive form of behaviour, not least because it is accompanied by an emotional reaction. Yet it is unclear whether the practical significance of insight really corresponds to its psychological reputation, because insight seems to be a relatively uncommon phenomenon. The significance of ordinary automatic forms of restructuring without the emotional overtones should not be underestimated. It may be that insight is just an important special case.

The best-known research on insight in the psychology of chess was carried out by de Groot (1965) and Tikhomirov and Vinogradov (1970). In his *Thought and Choice in Chess* de Groot (1965, p. 281) interpreted insight as a solution method, or the method of thought. It is not clear whether insight, which appears to be a highly automatic process and does not depend on the will, can be taken as a method. Insight should instead be considered as a form of restructuring that is associated with emotional processes.

Tikhomirov and Vinogradov (1970) demonstrated one process of this kind. They registered the galvanic skin response (GSR) of their

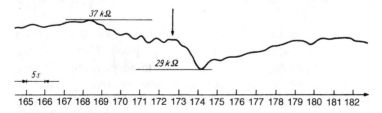

Figure 6.13 Galvanic skin response reactions in a moment of insight
Source: Tikhomirov and Vinogradov (1970)

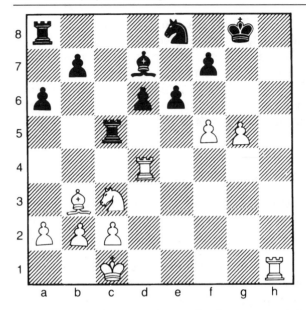

Ep1. f6 R × g5, Rdh4 N × f6, and Black loses a rook. Is there anything else for Black? . . . The same idea all the time, f6 R × g5, Rdh4.
Ep2. Wow!! Kf8 and the rook is able to parry the threat. Good grief . . . Well, it is necessary to start from the beginning. So, if Nd5 and if e × d5, then f6 and next Rdh4.

Figure 6.14 Insight

subjects and they found an example of a strong 'aha' experience with concurrent changes in GSR (see Figure 6.13). The protocols and the experiment by Tikhomirov and Vinogradov (1970) provide some support to the surprise aspect of insight. It seems to cause an orientation reaction, which has some effect on the physiological system as well.

It may be argued that insightful combinations are surprising because they require the restructuring of plans. They break one apperceived problem subspace in order to adopt another. Instead of standard information, surprising new information must be encoded, and the stimulus encoding is changed even though the objective stimulus remains the same.

Figure 6.14 presents a case of insight. It is one of the few absolutely clear cases of classic insight in the collection of protocols I have obtained during the past fifteen years, and therefore it is worth presenting.

The shift of the episode is very fast and the emotional 'aha' experience is also strong. The player clearly knows even before having checked all the variations that he or she has very probably found the solution. In fact, the player is not able to close all branches, but is intuitively certain about the right solution and selects the move. He or she has understood that Nd5 blockades the rook, and therefore all the previous calculations that have been refuted by the rook get a new wind.

In this particular case the insight is caused by the ability to remove at a stroke all the obstacles to the solution. The problem had developed to the point that this last piece of knowledge could allow everything to fall into place. The tension and uncertainty of the search seems to disappear very rapidly, and possibly this relief is

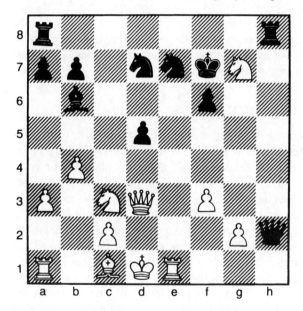

Rook takes e7 would appear as very promising. K takes e7. (*Experimenter*: What do you think?) I think N × d5+, which is very simple. One could play Ne5. Well, one could play R × e7 K × e7. If one plays Q × d5 after that . . . One could also play R × e7, Qg6 . . . then Qe5 and it is unclear . . . [. . .] I just keep repeating those continuations . . .

Figure 6.15 Ordinary shifts in a grandmaster protocol

the cause of the emotional reaction, which is so characteristic of all insights (Figure 6.13).

As I mentioned, the position shown in Figure 6.14 gave rise to one of the few classic cases of insight in all my collected protocols. Normally protocols are full of episodic and mental space shifts with no 'aha' experience (Figure 6.15). The logic of ordinary shifts was considered earlier. The motivation for an ordinary shift in apperceived representation is a failure to reach a good goal. When closing does not succeed, people are apt to restructure. However, the mechanisms of selecting mental spaces, and their ordering, for example, seem to be vital, but little-known, problems.

Newell and Simon (1972) argue that base moves in subjective search spaces – that is, the first moves in an episode – are independent. They also seem to suggest that people often begin with the most distinctive continuation. The experiments with smothered mate by Saariluoma (1990b) seem to suggest the same. Yet we do not know much about the order of processing. Even de Groot's (1965) progressive deepening seems to offer only a partial description. It looks as though we have paid too much attention to insight and all too little to ordinary restructuring.

COGNITIVE ERRORS IN CHESS

If a player is actively thinking in a wrong mental space, restructuring is crucial for finding a solution. The human attentional system prevents subjects from simultaneously analysing alternative mental spaces. Only by restructuring can the right mental space be found, and without restructuring the problem-solving process ends in an error. This means that restructuring is relevant not only for finding good moves but also in errors. Consequently, the role of subjective search space processing in cognitive errors must be considered.

The size of subjective search spaces and mental spaces is the first factor having an impact on errors. If chess players have a large capacity, they certainly make fewer errors, but capacity is not the only explanation for cognitive errors in chess. It is argued that experts are able to store a large number of task-necessary elements in their working memory and therefore they are able to find the solution or construct the required representation (Anderson *et al.* 1985, Johnson-Laird 1983). Though this explanation deals with one important aspect of cognitive errors, it leaves out the internal organization of mental spaces.

Careful analysis of the errors in normal competitive chess games and protocols shows, however, that the working memory load can hardly be the only source of cognitive errors in chess. The memory load required for storing the solution path is simply too low for errors to be explained by memory overload. The imaging interference must also be more a casual than a systematic reason for cognitive errors, because imaging interference-like factors are normally very firmly under control in competitive chess.

Saariluoma (1992b) presented an analysis of four hundred chess games at four different levels by Grandmaster Rantanen. In these analyses the main attention was paid to the loss of pieces, and the number of plies between the error move and the capture of the piece was coded. The errors were divided into four categories. The first category (I) contains all the errors in which the opponent could take material in his next move. In the second category of tactical errors (II), a player had made a move that led to material losses in two of his opponent's moves, or a move which missed the corresponding opportunity. In the third category (III), the limit was four moves, and in the fourth category were classified all the tactical errors in which the material loss took more than four moves (see Table 6.1). Even the strongest grandmasters made at least one tactical error per game, but in the lowest group players made six or more tactical errors per game.

The large number of small tactical errors is inconsistent with the working memory explanation. The incidence of one or two blunders is far too low to be explained by a simple limited-capacity working memory theory, which would claim that the memory load of the solution surpasses the natural limit of working memory. Anyone can

Table 6.1 Number of errors of four types in four skill groups per 100 games (I = something lost forcibly in one move, II = in two moves, III = in three moves and IV in four or more moves)

| | Player's ELO rating Categories of tactical errors | | | |
	I	II	III	IV
>2500	3	8	21	36
2200–2500	24	31	44	66
1700–1900	67	107	71	68
<1500	162	223	145	105

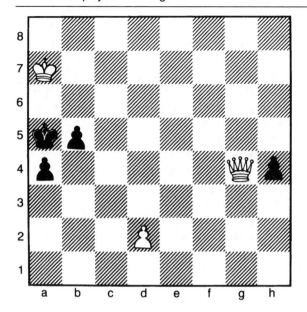

Figure 6.16 A very simple two-move mate (Qd1)

keep one ply in working memory, if it is noticed. The analysis of the protocols also showed that subjects do not necessarily fail because the memory load was too large, but because they do not abstract the right mental space or because they fail to close it (Saariluoma 1992b).

If one thinks of a chess problem in which the subject must find a mate in two moves, the final solution path is clearly within the working memory capacity limit, and subjects can use some form of external memory aid (i.e. the chessboard), yet still the problems may be very difficult.

In Figure 6.16 there is a nice but rather simple mate. The final solution path is just two moves, but there are so many possible mental spaces that the solution may be difficult to find. This is not necessarily because the load is high, but because the main space is strange, and the more obvious hypothetical moves blockade access to the correct space. The problem contains hypotheses that are simply illusory opportunities.

Working memory capacity as such cannot be an exhaustive explanation for cognitive errors in chess players' thinking. It is always necessary to take into account the apperceptive mechanisms that control mental space operations. The task-necessary decisions, the abstraction of the mental spaces, and their closing are at least as important reasons for errors in chess as is working memory capacity (Saariluoma 1992b).

Cognitive errors are not only caused by ignorance or working memory capacity deficits; subjective search space shifting mechanisms are also essential. Active mental spaces prevent the activation and thus prevent the study of the alternative spaces. Thus a consequence of investing resources in one mental space may be cognitive error. By investing in a bad idea, it is possible to blockade a better idea, which in principle could be solvable.

CONCEPTUAL RESTRUCTURING

Restructuring is essential in chess players' selective thinking. Indeed, it is the only way to avoid the negative consequences of selectivity. The basic reason for restructuring is the players' inability to close a mental space. This means that a player is unable to prove that the path from the initial position to the goal position is forced and that his or her opponent cannot find better alternatives, from the opponent's point of view, than the goal position. It may be that the restructuring is also caused by dissatisfaction with the goal. The need to search for the best moves is characteristic of high-level chess.

The phenomenon of restructuring has been known for a long time. Köhler (1917/1957) in his classic study on the mentality of apes brought restructuring into the very forefront of thinking research. Even though the Gestalt psychologists and others have discussed the problem, the position adopted here is essentially different from theirs.

The basic difference between my position and that of Gestaltists is clear. Gestaltists concentrated on restructuring as a perceptual phenomenon. If we exclude some parts of the late work of Duncker (1945) and Wertheimer (1945), restructuring was, to the Gestaltists, a change in the perceptual field (Ohlsson 1992). This becomes apparent in the way they constructed their experiments so that they were semantically as empty as possible and all elements of the problem situation were as fully visible as possible (Koffka 1935, Köhler 1917/1957). Especially problematic from the current point of view was the Gestaltists' inability to make a distinction between percepts and deeper representations.

The Gestaltists' position is not precise, because it does not take into account the most basic reasons for restructuring. It neglects the representational changes that take place on a level deeper than the perceptual level. Perception at the object level may be unchanged, as it usually is in chess, but still the conceptual representation may change dramatically.

Another difference between the Gestaltists' position and the current view concerns the importance of insight. To Gestaltists, insight was the most important form of restructuring. It was to them a method or form of learning that should lead to the best results. Here insight is regarded more as a special case which, because of its rarity, is not of prime importance. Any shift in the representation must be considered equally carefully. The change need not be followed by strong emotions. It may be very fast, automatic and routine. Furthermore, it may lead to a false hypothesis rather than the solution. Restructuring is a much wider notion than insight.

A much improved theory of restructuring was suggested by Ohlsson (1984a,b, 1992). Though he 'revisits' Gestaltists, he makes very clear representational assumptions and is critical about the Gestaltists' perceptualism. The importance of making the distinction between conceptual representations and percepts is obvious in his discussion of restructuring. The former approach very naturally opens up the multilayered structure of conceptual representations.

The higher level of deduction rules and the lower level of content-specific elements of representation work co-operatively to find the solution. It is true, as the Gestaltists argue, that thinking often causes dramatic changes in the perceptual world (Köhler 1917/1957, Ohlsson 1984a, b, 1992). However, the perceptual changes are only a symptom, not the thing itself. The changes in the contents of mind are essential and the changes in the perceptual field are secondary consequences of representational changes.

Chess players' selective thinking involves constant restructuring, as can be observed in the protocols. In restructuring, none of the pieces is moved, which means that the basic stimulus remains the same. Eye movement studies have shown that people fixate selectively on a chessboard, and when the position is changed, as in the Charness and Reingold (1992) study, the centre of their fixation changes too. Though we do not have any direct evidence at the moment, the results very strongly suggest that subjects seek information from the chessboard differently before and after restructuring.

Be that as it may, the refocusing of eye movements is an indirect measure, because eye movements are determined by the conceptual representation. Strong intermediate imagery use is commonly found in chess and the content of imagery manipulation must be conceptually controlled (Saariluoma 1990a). Therefore, the function of the eye movements is to find external support for the use of mental imagery. In blindfold chess no percepts are needed at all and thus an approach which reduces chess players' thinking to the mechanisms of perception is an oversimplification.

This is why it is justifiable to argue that representational changes are essential in restructuring, and that the changes in the perceptual field are secondary. It may be that we can draw some conclusions on the basis of the changes in the perceptual field, but no real understanding can be achieved about restructuring in chess unless the main attention is directed at conceptual representation and its transformations. Concepts, not percepts, are the key to human cognitions, and restructuring is in the first place a change in conceptual representation.

RESTRUCTURING IN SELECTIVE THINKING

Apperception is not the only process essential in selective thinking; restructuring is equally necessary. Apperception integrates information into mental spaces, and in so doing it makes extensive use of content-specific principles in the integration of information. Restructuring acts as a test of the apperceived mental spaces, and the logical control structures shift apperception from a failed mental space to another mental space that might be more successful.

This means that information selection is a two-level process. On the one hand hypotheses are constructed, but on the other hand these hypotheses must be tested. Selection without proper testing leads to errors. Indeed, the attitude that apperceived mental spaces are not properly tested we often call carelessness or sloppiness. It is not sufficient to select the contents of apperceived mental spaces; it is necessary to select between the mental spaces as well.

The two-level selection process is apparent in the protocols. Chess players generate episodes. Some of these clearly have the same 'deep' structure: that is, the same mental space with small variations. However, some of the episodes clearly originate from different mental spaces. To control the generation of mental spaces the mind needs apperception and to control the generation of different mental spaces restructuring is needed.

Both apperception and restructuring are broad 'umbrella' terms for different types of cognitive processes. At the moment we probably understand only a fraction of these mechanisms. Much work is needed to learn how the control takes place. This is difficult work because so much of the processing is unconscious, but it is necessary because the recovery of the unconscious mechanisms is absolutely necessary if progress is to be made in the psychology of thinking.

Chapter 7

Wider perspectives
Capacity, contents and thought

Conceptual analysis showed that selectivity is a term that has two meanings in the psychology of thinking. On the one hand selective information processing in thinking may refer to the capacity of the processing system; on the other hand it may allude to content-specific information selection. Both types of selective processes are very real in chess players' thinking and their effects can be demonstrated experimentally. Yet the two types of selectivity reflect very different types or levels of information processing.

Neisser (1976) made the conceptual distinction between negative and positive selection. By negative selection he referred to filtering and other mental processes that acted to exclude the irrelevant information. By positive selection Neisser meant processes in which the centre of attention is constructed. In contrast to filtering, construction should be considered as the basic process. The two types of selectivity found by studying chess players' thinking substantially elaborate on Neisser's (1976) ideas and provide a new basis for considering the two types of selective information processing.

Capacity-based information selection is a form of negative selectivity. The selectivity is found when the system is overloaded with the information needed to perform a task. People are either unable to attend to or to remember the information required by experimenters. The consequence of overloading is that semantically random errors appear. These may comprise small lapses or they may reflect an inability to perform the task, coupled with a total collapse of the representational system.

One reason for using the attribute negative as a descriptor of capacity-based selection derives from its semantically random character. Of course, non-semantic stimulus organization is often important, but the absence of semantically explainable effects makes the underlying process look random. Recency and primacy in list learning, for example, are important predictors of the probability of remembering an item. However, it is merely the location of the item in the list that is important. The contents of the items do not have any significance at this level. Although the semantic organization within a list is important, the recall probability depends not on the meaning but on the position in the list (Postman and Phillips 1965).

The content-specific selectivity has properties of positive selection. The elements in representations are picked out on the basis of their semantic properties. Each element to be associated with the representational structure must have certain semantic properties. The selected elements must make sense and belong together. Other elements are left out because they are irrelevant, and not because they would surpass some mechanical level.

The cognitive errors in content-specific selection are senseful. They arise because people represent the reality in a semantically non-optimal manner. This means that they have the wrong idea about what would be the best way of representing the task. Mostly the ways in which they represent reality are defensible only if their premises can be accepted. This means that we can understand why the errors arose, but only when we know what assumptions subjects made when constructing the representations. This is why we also think that content-specific cognitive errors are senseful or make sense.

The previous chapters have demonstrated the relevance of the two types of selectivity in chess players' information processing. Research on attention and memory demonstrated that capacity is an essential factor in explaining chess players' thinking. Lack of capacity explains why people construct relatively small representations. The capacity research provided information about automatization and chunking-type mechanisms, which allow experts to circumvent some of the negative effects of capacity.

The apperception and restructuring chapters demonstrated the reality of content-specific selectivity. The complex semantic and logical mechanisms explain how people can integrate relevant information into representations and modify them in a rational manner. There is no way one could reduce capacity or content-specific selectivity or vice versa, and thus they are two genuinely different types of selectivity.

The fact that capacity was essential in memory research and content-specific selectivity was found in apperception research does not mean that memory or attention would necessarily be capacity-oriented processes. Semantic memory research, for example, could entail content-specific aspects. Nevertheless, the tradition in chess psychology is capacity oriented and this is why capacity problems are dealt with mainly in the chapters on attention and memory.

The outcome of the analysis is clear. Capacity and content are postulates that refer to very different attributes of human information processing. Capacity cannot be explained in terms of contents, and contents cannot be reduced to capacity. Moreover, the two different types of selectivity seem to be linked with some of the most fundamental properties of human mind.

CAPACITY AND STATIC RESTRAINTS OF THOUGHT

In order to elaborate on the analysis, it is important to introduce a new concept, that of restraint. Any general factors, positive or negative, that impose limits on information processing may be called restraint. Restraint is thus a common term for all factors that cause errors in thinking, and prevent human problem solvers from finding effective solutions. This leads them to suboptimal or incorrect paths in their search. This is why the analysis of restraints is one of the main and constant goals for the psychology of human problem solving.

The point in introducing this new concept is simple. Capacity and content represent different types of restraints. While capacity with all the associated phenomena is a static restraint, which means that we do not know of a means to change it, content is a dynamic restraint and it changes with learning, the nature of the task, and cultural development. From this viewpoint, capacity and contents are two highly different notions, and this explains much about the methodological differences demanded in researching these two aspects of human cognition.

The basic cognitive limits behind capacity-based selection provide the best knowledge we have about the static restraints on thought. Human attentional capacity is one unit, unless actions are highly automatized or modularized (Broadbent 1958, James 1890). The human working memory can store only a few pieces of unintegrated information or carry out a few simultaneous tasks

(Atkinson and Shiffrin 1968, Baddeley 1983, 1986, 1990). There is no reason to believe that these basic restraints on human information processing could be changed or have changed very much for a long time. There is no evidence that humans have essentially improved the basic capacity of their attention or working memory over the centuries. The magical number seven was known in antiquity, and the need for mnemonics seem to have been very much the same thousands of years ago as it is today (Miller 1956, Yates 1966).

The ancient texts and fragments that discuss cognitive problems are ultimately very similar to our conceptions and provide no hint suggesting that the attention or memory functions of ancient Greeks were very different from ours. Ancient theories of memory contain nothing which would suggest that people remembered things differently (Aristotle 453–449BC, Freeman 1946). Indeed, the attentional capacity could only have decreased, because it is just 1 unit even today. Any substantial change in working memory capacity is for similar reasons very improbable.

Research on expertise raises another point concerning static restraints of thought. The basic capacity does not change with training. However, the available mechanisms can be used more effectively when information and experience increase. Although the development of chess skill greatly improves a chess master's ability to cope with the limitations of attention and memory, it never alters the basic limits. Experts simply learn to avoid the restraints by automatization and chunking, and no sign of improved general processing capacity can be found (Chase and Simon 1973a, b, Miller 1956, Schneider et al. 1984).

The improvement of chess skill does not make chess players' information processing immune to secondary task interference. Visuo-spatial and central executive interference tasks affect masters as well as novices (Bradley et al. 1987, Robbins et al., in preparation, Saariluoma 1991a, 1992a). The memory subsystems are not able to increase their basic processing capacity even though skills may improve.

The basic attentional capacity also seems to remain the same even when chess skill increases. Djakov et al. (1926) were able to find evidence which showed that chess players' basic attentional capacity was in no way different from that of non-chess players (Saariluoma 1984, 1985). In addition, if the basic attentional capacity had changed with improved skill, chess masters would very probably generate more than one problem subspace at a time, because the parallel processing of problem subspaces would greatly improve the speed of processing.

Static restraints do not prevent learning, but they impose limits on it. Hence, human processing may improve, though the basic capacity remains immutable. The human information processing system has means to circumvent the limits of static restraints. This does not mean that they could avoid the static restraints at will, because the mechanisms for this circumvention are themselves relatively stable. Somewhat paradoxically, the cognitive mechanisms imposing the limits on mind provide mechanisms to avoid some of the problems caused by the limits.

The human capacity to think depends on the ability to represent information in memory. When it is necessary, expert chess players are able to construct wider mental spaces, as has been argued by Charness (1981a, b) and Holding (1985, 1992a, b), though a wider search is not always necessary (de Groot 1965, Saariluoma 1990a). This means that the development of skill slowly reduces the restraints imposed by the capacity of human memory.

The main mechanism in avoiding memory restrictions is chunking. People are able to organize into chunks the material they wish to remember. Sometimes chunks may be very elementary and mechanistic. They may be strings of logically unconnected elements, as in the case of telephone numbers, but sometimes much more complex meaningful systems of relations are required (e.g. Anderson 1983, Black and Bower 1979, Chase and Simon 1973b).

In chess not all the details of the structure of chunks are known. Some elements such as pieces, their attributes and chess-specific relations are well known (Chase and Simon 1973a, b, Saariluoma 1984). Much less is known about the possible higher-level organization of chess memory. Goldin's (1978a, b, 1979) results as well as the work of Freyhof et al. (1992) or Pfau and Murphy (1988) support the idea of possible higher-level coding, but no precise description has been achieved so far.

As with chunking, human attention is limited by the immutable basic capacity of attention. However, the learning of visual-feature systems greatly improves processing speed. Skilled chess players are much faster in detecting checks or other threats, and they also make fewer errors in their thinking as their processing speed and accuracy improve.

Very little hope can be offered that the basic mechanisms used to avoid the capacity limits could be any more dynamic. It is evident that the roots of the static constraints lie in the biological mechanisms of the human brain. Thus they must evolve genetically, if they are to evolve at all. This means that the static restraints are a fact of life and we must learn to live with them.

APPERCEPTION AND DYNAMIC CONSTRAINTS

Since static restraints cannot be changed, people must learn to select the contents of their thought properly. Fortunately, very different pieces of information can be represented with the same capacity. Some contents are more important than others, and people who are able to find more effective contents for their thoughts are also able to select a better way of acting. In this way an intrinsically static mechanism may create the basis for the whole dynamism of human cultural and social evolution.

Chunking and improved pattern discrimination, which are consequences of learning, provide means for overcoming the low-level restraints. Much more advanced dynamic restraints can be found in the contents of thought. They depend on the level and the contents of the conceptual knowledge in an individual's mind. These are restraints that not only limit the individual's ability to find solutions but also affect the whole culture.

Apperception is abstraction of mental representations or, as in chess, of mental spaces. Of course, mental spaces are one type of representation. These spaces can be represented one at a time, and therefore they often blockade one another, since many chess positions offer a multitude of possible mental spaces. Discovery and creativity in chess are very much the ability to bring about new mental spaces in situations that earlier were abstracted differently.

If a single move is different from others in a long series of moves, this difference may be very important. In chess, very small things are decisive, and this is why abstraction of mental spaces is so difficult. A single poorly founded assumption may prevent a player from finding the best move. The history of opening theory, in particular, is full of examples of lost opportunities and brilliant improvements.

Of course, it is not always absolutely necessary to find the best possible moves, because optimal or 'good enough' moves may be sufficient (Reti 1933). However, the better or the more truthful are the mental spaces a player is able to abstract, the better is the quality of his or her game and the better the results that player may achieve.

Indeed, the difference between strong and very strong players often lies in small details. Overlooking one apparently insignificant move may lead to serious difficulties and eventually to the loss of a game.

The spatial logic of mental spaces and the capacity limits of human attention prevent players from searching more than one mental space at a time. Since there is no essential difference between beginners and experts in the basic capacity, the information content of the mental spaces is decisive (de Groot 1965). But the content depends on the conceptual knowledge that expert chess players have learned or found out for themselves.

Research into the knowledge base of chess experts has shown that chess players use different kinds of information in their thinking. Much of the knowledge contains named or unnamed patterns of pieces (Chase and Simon 1973a, b, Simon and Chase 1973). Much of it is verbal knowledge from the rules of the right conduct of game to historical facts and lay psychological assumptions concerning the opponent (Pfau and Murphy 1988, Reti 1933). It is possible that verbal knowledge may often be associated with pattern knowledge. 'Isolated queen's pawn', 'hanging pawns' or 'supported passed pawn', for example, are not just verbal concepts, and any good chess player certainly has a standard pattern corresponding to these concepts in memory.

Since both pattern and rule information is used to classify positions and to abstract problem subspaces, they together form the conceptual knowledge base of chess players. One should notice, however, that the amount of chess-specific knowledge is not in itself sufficient, though its content is decisive. It is not enough to know a great deal; it is important to know the right things. This was shown by Gruber and Strube's (1989) paper, in which they demonstrated how chess masters and problemists differ in their ability to solve chess problems. There is, of course, a considerable amount of transfer, as has been demonstrated by the grandmaster John Nunn, with his excellent performance in world championship chess problem-solving competitions. On the other hand, Pauli Perkonoja, who is probably the most successful chess problem solver over the past two decades, has never sought to achieve master status in game chess.

Apperception research suggests that it is not enough to work hard and acquire a great deal of knowledge about chess. It is necessary to know the right things. It is not sufficient to have ideas; it is vitally important to have the right ideas. Capacity-oriented research too easily focuses on the amount of information and neglects its contents. Dynamic constraints on thought are qualitative.

THINKING WITH CONCEPTS

The distinction between different types of selectivity and, even more so, the new way of looking at content-specific selectivity open new perspectives for research into complex problem solving and thinking. Apperception as the process unifying different semantic contents in a senseful manner is a central concept for this new look. When we understand apperception, we understand the most vital process in thinking. We understand how thinking selects the essential from the inessential.

Apperception is not perception, though it co-operates and controls the contents of perceptual representation. The reason is simple. Apperception is in no way stimulus-bound and apperceived representations need not be in any way connected to the stimulus environment. Direct perception is thus not necessary for apperception. Paradoxically, apperception is needed to understand what is perceived or attended, and thus apperception is necessary in perceiving.

Gestaltists understood very clearly that the perceptual field must be divided into a figure and ground (Koffka 1935, Köhler 1917/ 1957). Later this idea played an important role in defining attention (Kahneman 1973). However, Gestaltists had very little idea about why perceptual fields were selected as they were. By this I mean that perceptual fields always have contents and they always represent just one possible interpretation of reality. The cognitive mechanism behind this selection process belongs to the psychology of apperception. Since the Gestaltists were not interested in this concept their theories could not seek answers to questions concerning the semantics of perceptual field selection.

Apperception is a conceptual process. If apperceiving were a process organizing only the perceptual information, it could be called conceptual perception. However, the main function of apperception is to organize semantic elements into senseful and self-consistent wholes. Thus it need not be related to perceptual stimulus, or the relation may be very strongly conceptually mediated.

If we think of scientific work, for example, the thoughts are very often only indirectly related to the perceptual environment. The observations are instrumented, and series of numbers derived from apparatus may signify very different things, from atoms and galaxies to mind and emotions. Often the required perceptual information is collected over long periods of time and it may have been collected by people who had no direct connection with the thinking scientist. This conceptual mediation and the processes of constructing the mediated representations deserve much more research.

The restructuring research and memory research illustrate that the representational systems may contain different levels of information from very low-level patterns and images to high-level logical principles. While the former are highly content specific and domain dependent, the latter are practically context free. This system of superimposed conceptual layers makes all the research into apperception, conceptual mediation and representations much more complicated. But this complexity is typical of all representation.

Even in everyday thinking, people use complex concepts. These concepts are not at all necessarily linguistic concepts. They do not necessarily have a name or any other semiotic symbol attached. They are just models learned from parents or peers or experiences of life. A chess player has some 100,000 chess-specific patterns in mind, but no language has nearly 100,000 chess words. This means that our intuition at its lowest level is built on pattern knowledge, and any verbal control is minimal.

On the other hand, we are able to use this knowledge to apperceive representations. We are able to combine them in a senseful manner. No doubt logic and other higher-order conceptual representations have a role in ensuring self-consistency. How the elements are associated with representations and how the representations are associated will undoubtedly remain an important problem for the psychology of thinking for some time to come.

If our representations are conceptual, how do we know that they are right? In fact, we do not know. We are very prone to error, because we are unable to represent the situations correctly. Eyes are bad witnesses for a person who is unable to interpret what they see. Novices may look at a chessboard as long as they wish without understanding anything about the nuances of the situation. Similarly, a manager, a politician, an artist with no proper conceptual understanding of the task-specific situation may misinterpret a very clear visual message. None of us is free from the misconceptions. We all live in conceptual cages.

But if we live in conceptual cages, how can we overcome our limits? Expertise research has shown that training accumulates knowledge. On the other hand, research into the chess players' life-spans shows also that chess players do not necessarily become any better with increasing amounts of task-specific knowledge. It depends also what the knowledge is like and at what age it has been collected (Elo 1978). I fully agree with Hunt (1991) that this process of learning and knowledge accumulation is one of the central problems in complex problem-solving research. What we know today is that improved capability for solving problems depends on improved ability to apperceive the representations.

SKILL CULTURES

Concept formation is not only personal, it also has a very strong social aspect. New ideas may be discovered by some individuals, but much in the development of chess skill is culturally mediated. Hundreds of players actively study chess and every now and then they find new ideas. Other players adopt these ideas and develop them. When new ideas are found, the limits on the whole culture are pushed back.

In the Soviet championship Gurevitsh with the white pieces had beaten Sokolov by playing 0–0–0 in the position shown in Figure 7.1. At the same time in London, a world championship qualifying match was being played between Speelman and Short. Coincidentally, the wife of Speelman's second, Tisdall, had seen the game in a Norwegian newspaper. Before the *Bulletins of Soviet Championships* arrived in London Speelman was able to play the move against Short, achieving his first victory. The position had arisen regularly in competitive chess games before, but only now was long castling tried (*Suomen Shakki* 1/1989).

The constant need for novelties has made some top grandmasters make wide use of the assistance of other players. Kasparov (1987) tells vividly how much teamwork was used to support Karpov in his match against Korchnoi. He also pointed out some drawbacks of this system to the development of chess. The examples show overall, however, how necessary cultural creativity in modern chess is; even the best players have difficulties without their teams.

A subculture such as chess which is worldwide and based on a skill can be called a skill culture. Skill cultures are not local, they are globally organized. There are very few places in the world in

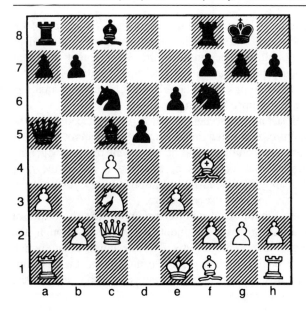

Figure 7.1 A victory by information transmission

which chess is not played, and there are chess clubs everywhere. The development of chess takes place in an international community that has its own rules and its own ways of behaving.

Chess is, of course, not the only skill culture in the world. Many if not all of our skills are organized around social groups of people who have devoted a part of their life to the advancement of a particular skill. Chess can serve as a paradigm case for the research of skill cultures. This research is vital, because skills are so vital in modern society. Moreover, in this way we can probably learn to understand better the social aspects of skills, especially the skill of thinking.

Of course, skill cultures may be very different. Milesian philosophy and Renaissance painting were much more local than the skill cultures of today. It is almost certain that chess differs from many other skill cultures. However, some surprising similarities can also be found. In postal chess, for example, a division of labour has very probably been used much like that in Renaissance painting. The leading chess players, like Renaissance artists, have concentrated on essential variations, while others have helped in working with the less essential ones.

At the moment, we know very little about the psychology of the development of a skill in a skill culture, which is very unfortunate, because our skill cultures are central in the development of human knowledge. Apperception plays a key role in skill cultures, and it is to be hoped that this complex and largely underresearched area will be investigated more thoroughly in the future.

It is not at all a rare phenomenon that a group of people or the whole skill culture is fixated and 'blind', and cannot properly interpret the task environment. The development of chess opening theory provides notable examples of this, but it is not the only example. Practically all scientific inventions open eyes to 'see' something that has not been 'seen' before.

Though chess is cultural, one must remember that the limits of human information processing cannot be changed, though the content of thought can. This is why it is the contents of human concepts that are decisive when we try to understand the development of skill cultures, for concepts form the connection between the individual and a skill culture.

Bibliography

Abrahams, G. (1951) *The Chess Mind*. Harmondsworth: Penguin Books.

Akin, O. (1980) *The Psychology of Architectural Design*. London: Pion.

Alba, J. W. and Hasher, L. (1983) 'Is memory schematic?' *Psychological Bulletin*, 93, 203–213.

Allport, D. A. (1975) 'The state of cognitive psychology'. *Quarterly Journal of Experimental Psychology*, 27, 141–152.

——— (1979) 'Conscious and unconscious cognition: a computational metaphor for the mechanism of attention and integration'. In L-G. Nilsson (ed.), *Perspectives on Memory Research: Essays in Honor of Uppsala University's 500th Anniversary*. Hillsdale, NJ: Erlbaum.

——— (1980a) 'Patterns and actions: cognitive mechanisms are content specific'. In G. Claxton (ed.), *Cognitive Psychology: New Directions*. London: Routledge & Kegan Paul, 26–64.

——— (1980b) 'Attention and performance'. In G. Claxton (ed.), *Cognitive Psychology: New Directions*. London: Routledge & Kegan Paul, 112–153.

——— (1989) 'Visual attention'. In M. I. Posner (ed.), *Foundations of Cognitive Science*. Cambridge, MA: MIT Press.

Allport, D. A., Antonis, B. and Reynolds, P. (1972) 'On the division of attention: a disproof of the single channel hypothesis'. *Quarterly Journal of Experimental Psychology*, 24, 225–235.

Anderson, J. R. (1976) *Language, Memory, and Thought*. Hillsdale, NJ: Erlbaum.

——— (1983) *The Architecture of Cognition*. Cambridge, MA.: Harvard University Press.

——— (1987) 'Skill acquisition: compilation of weak method problem solutions'. *Psychological Review*, 94, 192–210.

Anderson, J. R. and Bower, G. H. (1973) *Human Associative Memory*. Washington, DC: Winston.

Anderson, J. R. and Jeffries, R. (1985) 'Novice LISP errors: undetected losses of information from working memory'. *Human–Computer Interaction*, 22, 403–423.

Anderson, J. R., Farrell, R. and Sauers, R. (1984) 'Learning to program LISP'. *Cognitive Science*, 8, 87–130.

Apel, K. O. (1973) *Transformation der Philosophie I–II*. Frankfurt am Main: Surkamp. [Transformation of philosophy]

Aristotle (453–449BC) *On memory and recollection*. In W. S. Hett (transl.), *Aristotle in Twenty-three Volumes*. London: Heinemann.

Atkinson, R. and Shiffrin, R. (1968) 'Human memory: proposed system'. In K. W. Spence and J. T. Spence (eds.), *The Psychology of Learning and Motivation*, vol. 2. New York: Academic Press, 89–195.

Attneave, F. and Curlee, T. (1983) 'Locational representation in imagery: a moving spot task'. *Journal of Experimental Psychology: Human Perception and Performance*, 9, 20–30.

Baars, B. J. (1986) *The Cognitive Revolution*. New York: Guilford Press.

Bachmann, T. and Oit, M. (1992) 'Stroop-like interference in chess players' imagery: an unexplored possibility to be revealed by the adapted moving-spot task'. *Psychological Research*, 54, 27–31.

Baddeley, A. D. (1976) *The Psychology of Human Memory*. New York: Basic Books.

———— (1983) 'Working memory'. *Philosophical Transactions of the Royal Society*, London, B302, 311–324.

———— (1986) *Working Memory*. Cambridge: Cambridge University Press.

———— (1990) *Human Memory*. Hove: Erlbaum.

Baddeley, A. D. and Hitch, G. (1974) 'Working memory'. In G. Bower (ed.), *The Psychology of Learning and Motivation*, vol. 8. New York: Academic Press, 47–89.

Barron, F. H. (1988) 'Limits and extensions of equal weights in additive multiattribute models'. *Acta Psychologica*, 68, 141–152.

Bartlett, F. C. (1932/1977) *Remembering*. Cambridge: Cambridge University Press.

———— (1958) *Thinking*. London: Allen & Unwin.

Batchelder, W. H. and Bershad, NJ (1979) 'The statistical analysis of a Thurstonian model for rating chess players'. *Journal of Mathematical Psychology*, 19, 39–60.

Batchelder, W. H. and Simpson, R. S. (1988) 'Rating systems for human abilities'. *UMAP Module 698*. COMAP.

Baumgarten, F. (1930) *Wunderkinder* (Der 8 järige Schachwunderknabe). [Exceptionally talented children] Leipzig: Barth.

Berliner, H. (1974) 'Chess as problem solving'. Unpublished doctoral thesis, Carnegie-Mellon University.

Berlyne, D. E. (1965) *Structure and Direction of Thinking*. New York: Wiley.

Binet, A. (1893/1966) 'Mnemonic virtuosity: a study of chess players'. *Genetic Psychology Monographs*, 74, 127–164.

Black, J. B. and Bower, G. H. (1979) 'Episodes as chunks in narrative memory'. *Journal of Verbal Learning and Verbal Behavior*, 18, 309–318.

Blumefeld, B. M. (1948) 'K kharakteristike nyagladno-deistvennogo myshleniya' [On the character of perceptual actional thinking]. *Izvestiya APN RSFSR*, 13, 175–263.

Böök, E. E. (1967) *Shakkipakinoita*. [Chess stories] Helsinki: WSOY.

Botvinnik, M. M. (1984) *Computers in Chess: Solving Inexact Search Problems*. Berlin: Springer.

Bower, G. (1975) *Theories of Learning*. Englewood Cliffs: Prentice-Hall.

Bradley, A., Hudson, S., Robbins, T. and Baddeley, A. D. (1987) 'Working memory and chess'. Unpublished report, Cambridge, May 1987.

Broadbent, D. (1958) *Perception and Communication*. London: Pergamon Press.

―――― (1971) *Decision and Stress*. London: Academic Press.

―――― (1975) 'The magic number seven after twenty years'. In R. Kennedy and A. Wilkes (eds.), *Studies in Long Term Memory*. New York: Wiley, 253–287.

―――― (1980) 'The minimization of models'. In A. Chapman and D. Jones (eds.), *Models of Man*. Leicester: British Psychological Society.

Brooks, L. (1968) 'Spatial and verbal components in the act of recall'. *Canadian Journal of Psychology*, 22, 349–368.

Brown, J. (1958) 'Some tests on decay theory in immediate memory'. *Quarterly Journal of Experimental Psychology*, 10, 12–21.

Bruner, J., Goodnow, J. and Austin, G. (1956) *A Study of Thinking*. New York: Wiley.

Bryan, W. L. and Harter, N. (1899) 'Studies on the telegraphic language: the acquisition of a hierarchy of habits'. *Psychological Review*, 6, 345–375.

Bundesen, C. and Larsen, A. (1975) 'Visual transformation of size'. *Journal of Experimental Psychology: Human Perception and Performance*, 1, 214–220.

Bunge, M. (1967) *Scientific Research I–II*. Heidelberg: Springer.

Calderwood, B., Klein, G. A. and Randall, B. W. (1988) 'Time pressure and move quality in chess'. *American Journal of Psychology*, 101, 481–493.

Charness, N. (1974) 'Memory for chess positions: the effects of interference and input modality'. Unpublished Ph.D. thesis, Carnegie-Mellon University.

―――― (1976) 'Memory for chess positions: resistance to interference'. *Journal of Experimental Psychology: Human Learning and Memory*, 2, 641–653.

―――― (1977) 'Human chess skill'. In P. W. Frey (ed.), *Chess Skill in Man and Machine*. New York: Springer, 34–53.

―――― (1979) 'Components of skill in bridge'. *Canadian Journal of Psychology*, 33, 1–16.

―――― (1981a) 'Aging and skilled problem solving'. *Journal of Experimental Psychology: General*, 110, 21–38.

―――― (1981b) 'Search in chess: age and skill difference'. *Journal of Experimental Psychology: Human Perception and Performance*, 7, 467–476.

―――― (1981c) 'Visual short term memory and aging in chess players'. *Journal of Gerontology*, 36, 615–619.

―――― (1985) 'Aging and problem solving performance'. In N. Charness (ed.), *Aging and Human Performance*, New York: Wiley, 225–259.

―――― (1988) 'Expertise in chess, music, and physics: a cognitive perspective'. In L. K. Obler and D. A. Fein (eds), *The Exceptional Brain:*

Neuropsychology of Talent and Special Abilities. New York: Guilford Press, 399–426.

—— (1989) 'Expertise in chess and bridge'. In D. Klahr and K. Kotovsky (eds), *Complex Information Processing: The Impact of Herbert A. Simon*. Hillsdale, NJ: Erlbaum, 183–208.

—— (1991) 'Expertise in chess: the balance between knowledge and search'. In K. A. Ericsson and J. Smith (eds), *Toward a General Theory of Expertise*. Cambridge: Cambridge University Press, 39–63.

—— (1992) 'The impact of chess research on cognitive science'. *Psychological Research*, 54, 4–9.

Charness, N. and Reingold, E. (1992) 'Eye movement studies of problem solving in chess'. A presentation at the International Congress of Psychology, 18–25 July 1992, Brussels.

Chase, W. G. and Ericsson, K. A. (1981) 'Skilled memory'. In J. R. Anderson (ed.), *Cognitive Skills and their Acquisition*. Hillsdale, NJ: Erlbaum, 141–189.

—— (1982) 'Skill and working memory'. In G. Bower (ed.), *The Psychology of Learning and Motivation*, vol. 16. New York: Academic Press, 1–58.

Chase, W. G. and Simon, H. A. (1973a) 'Perception in chess'. *Cognitive Psychology*, 4, 55–81.

—— (1973b) 'The mind's eye in chess'. In W. Chase (ed.), *Visual Information Processing*. New York: Academic Press, 215–281.

Cherry, C. (1953) 'Some experiments on the recognition of speech with one and two ears', *Journal of the Acoustical Society of America*, 25, 975–979.

Chi, M. T. H. (1978) 'Knowledge structures and memory development'. In R. Siegler (ed.), *Children's Thinking: What Develops?* Hillsdale, NJ: Erlbaum, 73–96.

Chomsky, N. (1965) *Aspects of the Theory of Syntax*. Cambridge, MA.: MIT Press.

Church, R. M. and Church, K. W. (1977) 'Plans, goals, and search strategies for the selection of a move in chess'. In P. W. Frey (ed.), *Chess Skill in Man and Machine*. New York: Springer.

Clausewitz, Carl von (1832/1978) *On War*. Harmondsworth: Penguin Books.

Cleveland, A. A. (1907) 'The psychology of chess'. *American Journal of Psychology*, 18, 269–308.

Comrie, B. (1983) *Language Universals and Linguistic Typology*. Oxford: Basil Blackwell.

Cooke, N. J., Atlas, R. S., Lane, D. M. and Berger, R. C. (1993) 'Role of high-level knowledge in memory for chess positions'. *American Journal of Psychology*, 106, 321–351.

Cooper, L. A. and Shepard, R. N. (1973) 'Chronometric studies of the rotation of mental images'. In W. Chase (ed.), *Visual Information Processing*. New York: Academic Press, 75–176.

Craik, F. I. M. and Lockhart, R. S. (1972) 'The levels of processing: a framework for memory research'. *Journal of Verbal Learning and Verbal Behavior*, 11, 671–684.

Davidson, D. (1984) 'On the very idea of a conceptual scheme'. In D.

Davidson, *Inquiries into Truth and Interpretation*. Oxford: Clarendon Press.

Denis, M. (1991) *Image and Cognition*. New York: Harvester.

Descartes, R. (1637/1975) 'Discourse on method'. In *R. Descartes, Philosophical Works*, trans. E. S. Haldane and G. R. T. Ross. New York: Cambridge University Press.

Dewey, J. (1910) *How We Think*. New York: Macmillan.

Djakov, I. N., Petrovsky, N. B. and Rudik, P. A. (1926) *Psikhologiya Shakhmatnoi Igry*. [Psychology of the chess game] Moscow: Avtorov.

Doll, J. and Mayr, U. (1987) 'Intelligenz und Schachleistung: eine Untersuchung an Schachexperten' [Intelligence and chess performance: a study of chess experts] *Psychologische Beiträge*, 29, 270–289.

Dreyfus, H. L. (1972) *What Computers Can't Do*. New York: Harper.

—— (1992) *What Computers Still Can't Do: A Critique of Artificial Reason*. Cambridge, MA.: MIT Press.

Dreyfus, H. L. and Dreyfus, S. (1986) *The Mind over Machine*. Oxford: Basil Blackwell.

Duncker, K. (1945) 'On problem solving'. *Psychological Monographs*, vol. 270. Washington: American Psychological Association.

Egan, D. W. and Schwartz, B.J (1979) 'Chunking in recall of symbolic drawings'. *Memory and Cognition*, 7, 149–158.

Ellis, S. H. (1973) 'Structure and experience in the matching and reproduction of chess patterns'. Unpublished doctoral dissertation, Carnegie-Mellon University.

Elo, A. (1965) 'Age changes in master chess performances'. *Journal of Gerontology*, 20, 289–299.

—— (1978) *The Ratings of Chess Players: Past and Present*. London: Batsford.

Engle, R. W. and Bukstel, L. (1978) 'Memory processes among bridge players of different expertise'. *American Journal of Psychology*, 91, 673–689.

Ericsson, K. A. and Kintsch, W. (1994) *Long-term Working Memory*. ISC Technical Report no. 94–01. Boulder: University of Colorado.

Ericsson, K. A. and Polson, P. (1988) 'Experimental analysis of the mechanisms of memory skill'. *Journal of Experimental Psychology: Learning Memory and Cognition*, 14, 305–316.

Ericsson, K. A. and Simon, H. A. (1980) 'Verbal reports as data'. *Psychological Review*, 87, 215–251.

—— (1984) *Protocol Analysis*. Cambridge, MA: MIT Press.

Ericsson, K. A. and Smith, J. (1991) 'Prospect and limits of the empirical study of expertise'. In K. A. Ericsson and J. Smith (eds.), *Toward a General Theory of Expertise*. Cambridge: Cambridge University Press, 1–38.

Ericsson, K. A. and Staszewski, J. (1989) 'Skilled memory and expertise: mechanisms of exceptional performance'. In D. Klahr and K. Kotovsky (eds), *Complex Information Processing: The Impact of Herbert A. Simon*. Hillsdale, NJ: Erlbaum, 235–267.

Euwe, M. and Kramer, H. (1956) *Das Mittelspiel*. Hamburg: Schach-Archiv. [The middle game].

Evans, J. St. B. T. (1982) *The Psychology of Deductive Reasoning*. London: Routledge & Kegan Paul.

——— (1989) *Bias in Human Reasoning*. Hove: Erlbaum.

Fine, R. (1956) *The Psychology of the Chess Player*. New York: Dover.

——— (1965) 'The psychology of blindfold chess: an introspective account'. *Acta Psychologica*, 24, 352–370.

Fisk, A. D. and Lloyd, S. J. (1988) 'The role of stimulus-to-rule consistency in learning rapid application of spatial rules'. *Human Factors*, 30, 35–49.

Freeman, K. (1946) *A Companion to Presocratic Philosophers*. Oxford: Basil Blackwell.

French, P. A. and Sternberg, R. J. (1991) 'Skill related differences in game playing'. In R. J. Sternberg and P. A. Frey (eds), *Complex Problem Solving*. Hillsdale, NJ: Erlbaum, 343–381.

Frey, P. W. and Adesman, P. (1976) 'Recall memory for visually presented chess positions'. *Memory and Cognition*, 4, 541–547.

Freyhof, H., Gruber, H. and Ziegler, A. (1992) 'Expertise and hierarchical knowledge representation in chess'. *Psychological Research*, 54, 32–37.

Gadamer, H. G. (1975) *Truth and Method*. New York: Seabury.

Gibson (1941)

Gibson, E. J. (1969) *Principles of Perceptual Learning and Development*. Englewood Cliffs, NJ: Prentice-Hall.

Gibson, J. J. (1986) *The Ecological Approach to Visual Perception*. Hillsdale, NJ: Erlbaum.

Gilhooly, K. J. (1986) 'Individual differences in thinking aloud performance'. *Current Psychological Research and Reviews*, 40A, 328–334.

Gilhooly, K. J. and Green, A. J. K. (1988) 'The use of memory in experts and novices'. In A. M. Colley and J. R. Beech (eds.), *Cognition and Action in Skilled Behavior*. London: Elsevier.

Gilhooly, K., Wood, M., Kinnear, P. and Green, C. (1988) 'Skill in map reading and memory for maps'. *Quarterly Journal of Experimental Psychology*, 40A, 87–107.

Gobet, F. R. (1992) 'Learned helplessness in chess players: the importance of task similarity and the role of skill'. *Psychological Research*, 54, 38–43.

Gobet, F. and Simon, H. A. (1994a), 'Templates in chess recall memory: a mechanism for recalling several boards'. Complete Information Processing Working Paper no. 513.

——— (1994b) 'Expert chess memory: revisiting chunking hypothesis'. Comple Information Processing Working Paper no. 515.

Gold, A. and Opwis, K. (1992) 'Methoden zur empirischen Analyse von Chunks beim Reproduzieren von Schachstellungen' [Methods of empirical analysis of chunks in the reproduction of chess positions] *Sprache und Kognition*, 11, 1–13.

Goldin, S. (1978a) 'Memory for the ordinary: typicality effects in chess memory'. *Journal of Experimental Psychology: Human Learning and Memory*, 4, 605–616.

——— (1978b) 'The effects of orienting tasks on recognition of chess positions'. *American Journal of Psychology*, 91, 659–671.

——— (1979) 'Recognition memory for chess positions'. *American Journal of Psychology*, 92, 19–31.

Golz, A. and Keres, P. (1972) *Schönheit der Kombination*. [The beauty of combination] Berlin: Sportverlag.

de Groot, A. D. (1965) *Thought and Choice in Chess*. The Hague: Mouton.

—— (1966) 'Perception and memory versus thought: some old ideas and recent findings'. In B. Kleinmuntz (ed.), *Problem Solving*. New York: Wiley, 19–50.

Gruber, H. and Strube, G. (1989) 'Zweierlei Experten: Problemisten, Parteispieler und Novizen beim Lösen von Schachproblemen'. [Differences among experts: problemists, players and novices in the solving of chess problems] *Sprache und Kognition*, 8, 72–85.

Hanson, N. R. (1958) *Patterns of Discovery*. Cambridge: Cambridge University Press.

Hartston, W. R. and Wason, P. C. (1983) *The Psychology of Chess*. Batsford.

Hayes, J. (1981) *The Complete Problem Solver*. Philadelphia: Franklin Institute Press.

—— (1985) 'Three problems in teaching general skills'. In S. Chipman, J. Segal and R. Glaser (eds.), *Thinking and Learning Skills*, vol. 2. Hillsdale, NJ: Erlbaum.

Heuer, H. and Wing, A. M. (1984) 'Doing two things at once: process limitations and interactions'. In M. M. Smyth and A. M. Wing (eds), *The Psychology of Human Movement*. New York: Academic Press, 183–326.

Hintikka, K. J. (1969) 'Tieteen metodi analyyttisenä toimituksena' (The analytical method of science). In K. J. Hintikka, *Tieto on valtaa*. [Knowledge is power] Porvoo: WSOY.

Hobbes, Th. (1651) *Leviathan*. London: Dent.

Hochberg, J. (1970) 'Attention, organization, and consciousness'. In D. Mostofsky (ed.), *Attention: Contemporary Theory and Analysis*. New York: Appleton-Century-Crofts.

Hohlfeld, M. (1988) Schachliches Denken während ganzer Partien: Pilotstudie mittels der Methode des lauten Denkens. [Chess thinking during a whole game: a pilot study using the method of thinking aloud] Unpublished diploma work, University of Tübingen.

Holding, D. H. (1979) 'The evaluation of chess positions'. *Simulation and Games*, 10, 207–221.

—— (1985) *The Psychology of Chess Skill*. Hillsdale, NJ: Erlbaum.

—— (1989) 'Adversary problem solving by humans'. In K. Gilhooly (ed.), *Human and Machine Problem Solving*. London: Plenum Press, 83–122.

—— (1992a) 'Theories of chess skill'. *Psychological Research*, 54, 10–16.

—— (1992b) 'Search process vs. pattern structure in chess skill'. In B. Burns (ed.), *Percepts, Concepts and Categories*. Amsterdam: Elsevier.

Holding, D. H. and Pfau, H. D. (1985) 'Thinking ahead in chess'. *American Journal of Psychology*, 98, 421–424.

Holding, D. H. and Reynolds, R. I. (1982) 'Recall or evaluation of chess positions as determinants of chess skill'. *Memory and Cognition*, 10, 237–242.

Horgan, D. D. (1992) 'Children and chess expertise: the role of calibration'. *Psychological Research*, 54, 44–50.

Horgan, D. D. and Morgan, D. (1989) 'Chess expertise in children'. *Applied Cognitive Psychology*, 4, 109–128.

Hull, C. L. (1943) *Principles of Behavior*. New York: Appleton-Century-Crofts.

——— (1952) *A Behavior System*. New Haven, CT: Yale University Press.

Hunt, E. (1991) 'Some comments on study of complexity'. In R. J. Sternberg and P. A. Frey (eds), *Complex Problem Solving*. Hillsdale, NJ: Erlbaum, 343–381.

Hunt, E. and Love, T. (1972) 'How good can memory be?' In A. W. Melton and E. Martin (eds), *Coding Processes in Human Memory*. Washington, DC: Winston.

James, W. (1890) *The Principles of Psychology*. New York: Dover.

Johnson-Laird, P. (1983) *Mental models: Towards a Cognitive Science of Language, Inference, and Consciousness*. Cambridge, MA: Harvard University Press.

Johnson-Laird, P. and Byrne, R. (1991) *Deduction*. Hove: Erlbaum.

Jones, E. (1987) *Die Theorie der Symbolik und andere Aufsätze*. [The theory of symbolism and other writings] Frankfurt am Main: Atheneum.

Jungermann, H. (1983) 'Two camps of rationality'. In R. W. Scholz (ed.), *Decision Making under Uncertainty*. Amsterdam: Elsevier.

Kahneman, D. (1973) *Attention and Effort*. Englewood Cliffs, NJ: Prentice-Hall.

Kant, I. (1781/1966) *Critique of Pure Reason*, trans. M. Müller. New York: Anchor Books.

Kaplan, C. A. and Simon, H. A. (1990) 'In search of insight'. *Cognitive Psychology*, 22, 374–419.

Kasparov, G. (1987) *Unlimited Challenge*. Glasgow: Fontana.

Kinnear, P. and Wood, M. (1987) 'Memory for topographic contour maps'. *British Journal of Psychology*, 78, 395–402.

Klein, G. A. (1989) 'Recognition-primed decisions'. In W. R. Rouse (ed.), *Advances in Man–Machine System Research*, vol. 5.

Klein, G. A. and Peio, K. (1989) 'Use of prediction paradigm to evaluate proficient decision making'. *American Journal of Psychology*, 102, 321–339.

Koffka, K. (1935) *Principles of Gestalt Psychology*. New York: Harbinger.

Köhler, W. (1917/1957) *The Mentality of Apes*. Harmondsworth: Penguin.

Krogius, N. (1976) *Psychology in Chess*. New York: R.H.M. Press.

Kuhn, Th. (1962) *The Structure of Scientific Revolutions*. Chicago: University of Chicago Press.

La Berge, D. (1976) 'Perceptual learning and attention'. In W. Estes (ed.), *Handbook of Learning and Cognitive Processes*. Hillsdale, NJ: Erlbaum.

Lakatos, I. M. (1970) 'Falsification and the methodology of research programmes'. In I. Lakatos and A. Musgrave (eds), *Criticism and the Growth of Knowledge*. Cambridge: Cambridge University Press.

Lane, D. M. and Robertson, L. (1979) 'The generality of the levels of processing hypothesis: an application to memory for chess positions'. *Memory and Cognition*, 7, 253–256.

Lasker, E. (1947) *Lasker's Manual of Chess*. New York: Dover.

Laudan, L. (1977) *Progress and its Problems: Towards a Theory of Scientific Growth*. Routledge & Kegan Paul: London.

Lehman, H. (1953) *Age and Achievement*. Princeton, NJ: Princeton University Press.

Leibniz, G. (1704) *New Essays on Human Understanding*. Cambridge: Cambridge University Press.

Logie, R. H. (1986) 'Visuo-spatial processing in working memory'. *Quarterly Journal of Experimental Psychology*, 38A, 229–247.

Logie, R., Wright, R. and Decker, S. (1992) 'Recognition memory performance and residential burglary'. *Applied Cognitive Psychology*, 6, 109–123.

Lories, G. (1987) 'Recall of random and non random chess positions in strong and weak chess players'. *Psychologica Belgica*, 27, 153–159.

Luchins, A. (1942) 'Mechanization in problem solving: the effect of einstellung'. *Psychological Monographs*, 54, no. 248.

McKeithen, K., Reitman, J., Rueter, H. and Hirtle, S. (1981) 'Knowledge organization and skill differences in computer programmers'. *Cognitive Psychology*, 13, 307–325.

Mackworth, N. and Morandi, A. (1966) 'The gaze selects informative details within pictures'. *Perception and Psychophysics*, 2, 547–552.

Maier, N. R. (1930) 'Reasoning in humans I: On direction'. *Journal of Comparative Psychology*, 12, 181–194.

――― (1931) 'Reasoning in humans II: The solution of a problem and its appearance in consciousness'. *Journal of Comparative Psychology*, 12, 181–194.

Maltzman, I. (1955) 'Thinking from a behaviorist point of view'. *Psychological Review*, 62, 275–286.

Mandler, J. and Parker, R. (1976) 'Memory for descriptive and spatial information in complex pictures'. *Journal of Experimental Psychology: Human Learning and Memory*, 2, 38–48.

Marr, D. (1982) *Vision*. San Francisco: Freeman.

Mayer, R. E. (1983) *Thinking, Problem Solving, Cognition*. San Francisco: Freeman.

Miller, G. E. (1956) 'The magical number seven plus or minus two: Some limits on our capacity for processing information'. *Psychological Review*, 63, 81–97.

Miller, G. E., Galanter, E. and Pribram, K. (1960) *Plans and the Structure of Behavior*. New York: Holt.

Milojkovic, J. (1982) 'Chess imagery in novice and master'. *Journal of Mental Imagery*, 6, 125–144.

Montgomery, H. and Svensson, O. (1976) 'On decision rules and information processing strategies for choices among multiattribute alternatives'. *Scandinavian Journal of Psychology*, 17, 283–291.

Munzert, R. (1989) *Schachpsychologie*. (Chess psychology) Hollfeld: Beyer.

Mylers-Worsley, M., Johnston, W. and Simmons, M. (1988) 'The influence of expertise on X-ray image processing'. *Journal of Experimental Psychology: Learning Memory and Cognition*, 14, 553–557.

Nagel, E. (1961) *The Structure of Science: Problems in the Logic of Scientific Explanation*. London: Routledge & Kegan Paul.

Navon, D. (1989a) 'The importance of being visible: on the role of attention in a mind viewed as an anarchic intelligence system I. Basic tenets'. *European Journal of Cognitive Psychology*, 1, 191–213.

―――― (1989b) 'The importance of being visible: on the role of attention in a mind viewed as an anarchic intelligence system II. Application to the field of attention'. *European Journal of Cognitive Psychology*, 1, 215–238.

Neisser, U. (1963) 'Decision time without reaction time'. *American Journal of Psychology*, 76, 376–385.

―――― (1967) *Cognitive Psychology*. New York: Appleton-Century-Crofts.

―――― (1976) *Cognition and Reality*. San Francisco: Freeman.

―――― (1987) 'From direct perception to conceptual structure'. In U. Neisser (ed.), *Concepts and Conceptual Development: Ecological and Intellectual Factors in Categorization*. Cambridge: Cambridge University Press.

Neumann, O. (1984) 'Automatic processing: a review of recent findings and a plea for an old theory'. In W. Prinz and A. Sanders (eds.), *Cognition and Motor Processes*. Berlin: Springer.

―――― (1990) 'Visual attention and action'. In O. Neumann and W. Prinz (eds.), *Relationships between Perception and Action*. Berlin: Springer, 227–267.

Newell, A. (1973a) 'Production systems: models of control structures'. In W. G. Chase (ed.), *Visual Information Processing*. New York: Academic Press.

―――― (1973b) 'We cannot play Twenty Questions with nature'. In W. G. Chase (ed.), *Visual Information Processing*. New York: Academic Press.

―――― (1977) 'On the analysis of human problem solving'. In P. N. Johnson-Laird and P. C. Wason (eds.), *Thinking: Readings in Cognitive Science*. Cambridge: Cambridge University Press, 46–61.

―――― (1990) *Unified Theories of Cognition*. Cambridge, MA: Harvard University Press.

Newell, A. and Simon, H. A. (1963) 'GPS, a program that simulates human thought'. In E. Feigenbaum and J. Feldman (eds), *Computers and Thought*. New York: McGraw-Hill, 279–293.

―――― (1972) *Human Problem Solving*. Englewood Cliffs, NJ: Prentice-Hall.

―――― (1976) 'Computer science as empirical enquiry: symbols and search'. In J. Haugeland (ed.), *Mind Design*. Cambridge, MA: MIT Press, 35–66.

Newell, A., Shaw, J. and Simon, H. A. (1958) 'Elements of a theory of human problem solving'. *Psychological Review*, 65, 151–166.

―――― (1963) 'Chess playing programs and the problem of complexity'. In E. A. Feigenbaum and J. Feldman (eds), *Computers and Thought*. New York: McGraw-Hill, 39–70.

Norman, D. (1981) 'Categorization of action slips'. *Psychological Review*, 88, 1–15.

Norman, D. A. and Bobrow, D. G. (1975) 'On data-limited and resource-limited processes'. *Cognitive Psychology*, 7, 44–64.

Norman, D. A. and Shallice, T. (1986) 'Attention to action: willed and automatic control of behavior'. In R. J. Davidson, G. E. Schwartz and D. Shapiro (eds), *Consciousness and Self-regulation*, vol. 4. New York: Plenum Press.

Ohlsson, S. (1984a) 'Restructuring revisited I. Summary and critique of the Gestalt theory of problem solving'. *Scandinavian Journal of Psychology*, 25, 65–78.

––––––– (1984b) 'Restructuring revisited II. An information processing theory of restructuring and insight'. *Scandinavian Journal of Psychology*, 25, 117–129.

––––––– (1992) 'Information processing explanation of insight and related phenomena'. In M. T. G. Keane and K. Gilhooly (eds), *Advances in the Psychology of Thinking*, vol. 1. London: Harvester, 1–44.

Paivio, A. (1971) *Imagery and Verbal Processes*. New York: Holt.

––––––– (1986) *Mental Representations*. New York: Oxford University Press.

Payne, J. (1982) 'Contingent decision behavior'. *Psychological Bulletin*, 92, 382–402.

Peterson, L. R. and Peterson, M. J. (1959) 'Short term retention of individual items'. *Journal of Experimental Psychology*, 58, 193–198.

Pfau, H. D. and Murphy, M. D. (1988) 'The role of verbal knowledge in chess'. *American Journal of Psychology*, 98, 271–282.

Pfleger, H. and Treppner, G. (1987) *Chess: The Mechanics of Mind*. Marlborough: Crowood Press.

Piaget, J. (1952) *The Child's Concept of Number*. New York: Norton.

Polya, G. (1954) *How to Solve It*. Princeton, NJ: Princeton University Press.

Popper, K. R. (1959) *The Logic of Scientific Discovery*. London: Hutchinson.

––––––– (1972) *Objective Knowledge: An Evolutionary Approach*. Oxford: Clarendon Press.

Postman, L. and Phillips, L. (1965) 'Short term temporal changes in free recall'. *Quarterly Journal of Experimental Psychology*, 17, 132–138.

Rabbitt, P. (1978) 'Sorting, categorization and visual search'. In E. Carterette and M. Friedman (eds.), *Handbook of Perception*, vol. 9. New York: Academic Press.

––––––– (1984) 'The control of attention in visual search'. In R. Parasuraman and D. Davies (eds), *Varieties of Attention*. Orlando, FL: Academic Press.

Reitman, J. (1976) 'Skilled perception in Go: deducing memory structures from inter-response times'. *Cognitive Psychology*, 8, 336–356.

Reti, R. (1933) *Masters of the Chessboard*. London: Bell & Sons.

Reynolds, R. I. (1982) 'Search heuristics of chess players of different calibres'. *American Journal of Psychology*, 95, 383–392.

Robbins, T. W., Anderson, E. J., Barker, D. R., Bradley, A. C., Fearnyhough, R., Henson, R., Hudson, S. R. and Baddeley, A. (in preparation). *Working Memory in Chess*.

Rock, I. (1983) *The Logic of Perception*. Cambridge, MA: MIT Press.

Saariluoma, P. (1979) 'Shakinpelaajan ongelmanratkaisuprosessi' (Chess players' problem-solving process). Unpublished licenciate thesis, University of Turku.

────── (1984) 'Coding problem spaces in chess'. *Commentationes scientiarum socialium*, vol. 23. Turku: Societas Scientiarum Fennica.

────── (1985) 'Chess players' intake of task relevant cues'. *Memory and Cognition*, 13, 385–391.

────── (1989) 'Chess players' recall of auditorily presented chess positions'. *European Journal of Cognitive Psychology*, 1, 309–320.

────── (1990a) 'Chess players' search for task relevant cues: are chunks relevant?' In D. Brogan (ed.), *Visual Search*. London: Taylor & Francis.

────── (1990b) 'Apperception and restructuring in chess players' problem solving'. In K. J. Gilhooly, M. T. G. Keane, R. H. Logie and G. Erdos (eds), *Lines of thought: Reflections on the Psychology of Thinking*. Wiley: London, 41–57.

────── (1991a) 'Visuo-spatial interference and apperception in chess'. In M. Denis and R. Logie (eds), *Images in Cognition*. Elsevier: Amsterdam, 83–94.

────── (1991b) 'Aspects of skilled imagery in blindfold chess'. *Acta Psychologica*, 77, 65–89.

────── (1992a) 'Visuo-spatial and articulatory interference in chess players' information intake'. *Applied Cognitive Psychology*, 6, 77–89.

────── (1992b) 'Error in chess: apperception restructuring view'. *Psychological Research*, 54, 17–26.

────── (1994) 'Location coding in chess'. *Quarterly Journal of Experimental Psychology*, 47A, 607–630.

Saariluoma, P. and Hohlfeld, M. (1994) 'Chess players' long-range planning'. *European Journal of Cognitive Psychology*, 6, 1–22.

Schneider, W., Dumais, S. and Shiffrin, R. (1984) 'Automatic and controlled processing and attention'. In R. Parasuraman and D. Davies (eds), *Varieties of Attention*. Orlando, FL: Academic Press.

Sellars, W. (1956) 'Empiricism and the philosophy of mind'. In H. Feigl and M. Scriven (eds), *Minnesota Studies in the Philosophy of Science*, vol. 1. Minneapolis: University of Minnesota Press.

────── (1963) *Science, Perception, Reality*. London: Routledge & Kegan Paul.

Selz, O. (1913) *Ueber die Gesetze des geordneten Denkverlaufs*. [On the laws of organized thinking] Stuttgart: Spemann.

────── (1924) *Zur Psychologie des productiven Denkens und des Irritums*. [Psychology of productive thinking and erring.] Bonn: Cohen.

Shaffer, L. (1975) 'Multiple attention in continuous verbal tasks'. In P. Rabbitt and S. Dornic (eds), *Attention and Performance*, vol. 5. New York: Academic Press.

Shannon, C. E. (1950) 'Programming computers to play chess'. *Philosophical Magazine*, 41, 256–275.

Shepard, R. (1967) 'Memory for words, sentences and pictures'. *Journal of Verbal Learning and Verbal Behavior*, 1, 156–163.

Shepard, R. and Metzler, J. (1971) 'Mental rotation of three dimensional objects'. *Science*, 171, 701–703.

Shiffrin, R. M. (1976) 'Capacity limitations in information processing, attention and memory'. In W. K. Estes (ed.), *Handbook of Learning and Cognitive Processes*, vol. 4. Hillsdale, NJ: Erlbaum, 177–236.

Shiffrin, R. M. (1988) 'Attention'. In R. C. Atkinson, R. J. Herrnstein, G. Lindzey and R. D. Luce (eds), *Stevens' Handbook of Experimental Psychology*, vol. 2: *Learning and Cognition*. New York: Wiley, 731–811.

Shneiderman, B. (1976) 'Exploratory experiments in programmer behavior'. *International Journal of Computer and Information Sciences*, 5, 123–143.

Simon, H. A. (1956) 'Rational choice and the structure of the environment'. *Psychological Review*, 63, 129–138.

—— (1974a) 'How big is a chunk?' *Science*, 183, 482–488.

—— (1974b) 'The psychology of "losing move" in a game of perfect information'. *Proceedings of the National Academy of Sciences, USA*, 71, 2276–2279.

—— (1974c) 'Losing move: an information processing concept'. *SIGART Newsletter*, 48, 9–10.

—— (1976) 'The information storage system called human memory'. In M. Rosenzweig and E. Bennett (eds), *Neural Mechanisms of Learning and Memory*. Cambridge, MA: MIT Press.

—— (1979) 'Information processing models of cognition'. *Annual Review of Psychology*, 30, 363–396.

—— (1983) *Rationality in Human Affairs*. Stanford, Calif.: Stanford University Press.

Simon, H. A. and Barenfeld, M. (1969) 'Information-processing analysis of perceptual processes in problem solving'. *Psychological Review*, 76, 473–483.

Simon, H. A. and Chase, W. G. (1973) 'Skill in chess'. *American Scientist*, 61, 394–403.

Simon, H. A. and Gilmartin, K. (1973) 'A simulation of memory for chess positions'. *Cognitive Psychology*, 5, 29–46.

Skinner, B. F. (1957) *Verbal Behavior*. New York: Appleton-Century-Crofts.

Sloboda, J. (1976) 'Visual perception of musical notation: Registering pitch symbols in memory'. *Quarterly Journal of Experimental Psychology*, 28, 1–16.

Stanat, D. F. and McAllister, D. F. (1977) *Discrete Mathematics in Computer Science*. Englewood Cliffs, NJ: Prentice-Hall.

Standing, L. (1973) 'Learning 10,000 pictures'. *Quarterly Journal of Experimental Psychology*, 25, 207–222.

Stout, G. F. (1896) *Analytic Psychology*. New York: Macmillan.

Suppe, F. (1977) 'The search for philosophical understanding of scientific theories'. In F. Suppe (ed.), *The Structure of Scientific Theories*. Chicago: University of Illinois Press.

Thorndike, E. L. (1911) *Animal Intelligence*. New York: Macmillan.

Tikhomirov, O. K. (1988) *The Psychology of Thinking*. Moscow: Progress Publishers.

Tikhomirov, O. K. and Poznyanskaya, E. D. (1966) 'An investigation of visual search as a means of analysing heuristics'. *Soviet Psychology*, 5, 2–15.

Tikhomirov, O. K. and Terehov, V. A. (1967) 'Evristiki cheloveka' (Human heuristics). *Voprosy Psikhologii*, 13, 26–41.

Tikhomirov, O. K. and Vinogradov, Ye. E. (1970) 'Emotions in the function of heuristics'. *Soviet Psychology*, 8, 198–223.

Treisman, A. (1969) 'Strategies and models of selective attention'. *Psychological Review*, 76, 282–299.

Troitsky, A. A. (1968) *Three Hundred and Sixty Brilliant and Instructive End Games*. New York: Dover.

Tuomela, R. (1977) *Human Action and its Explanation*. Dordrecht: Reidel.

Turing, A. M. (1950) 'Computing machinery and intelligence'. *Mind*, 59, 433–450.

Tversky, A. and Kahneman, D. (1974) 'Judgement under uncertainty: heuristics and biases'. *Science*, 185, 1124–1131.

Uhlman, S. (1984) 'Visual routines'. *Cognition*, 18, 97–159.

van der Heijden, A. H. C. (1990) 'Visual information processing and selection'. In O. Neumann and W. Prinz (eds), *Relationships between Perception and Action*. Berlin: Springer, 203–226.

VanLehn, K. (1990) *Mind Bugs: The Origins of Procedural Misconceptions*. Cambridge, MA: MIT Press.

Vicente, K. J. (1988) 'Adapting the memory recall paradigm to evaluate interfaces'. *Acta Psychologica*, 69, 249–278.

Vicente, K. J. and de Groot, A. D. (1990) 'The memory recall paradigm: straightening out the historical record'. *American Psychologist*, 45, 285–287.

Wagenaar, W. (1988) *Paradoxes of Gambling Behavior*. Hove: Erlbaum.

Wason, P. C. and Johnson-Laird, P. (1972) *Psychology of Reasoning: Structure and Content*. London: Batsford.

Watkins, M. J. (1977) 'The intricacy of memory span'. *Memory and Cognition*, 5, 529–534.

Waugh, N. and Norman, D. (1965) 'Primary memory'. *Psychological Review*, 72, 89–104.

Weinert, F., Schneider, W. and Knopf, M. (1987) 'Individual differences in memory development across the life span'. *Max-Planck-Institute for Psychological Research: Preprint* 2/1987.

Wertheimer, M. (1945) *Productive Thinking*. Westport, Conn.: Greenwood.

Wilkins, D. E. (1979) 'Using patterns and plans to solve problems and control search'. Unpublished doctoral dissertation, Stanford University.

Wundt, W. (1880) *Logik*, vol. 1. Stuttgart: Ferdinand Enke.

Yarbus, A. (1967) *Eye Movements and Vision*. New York: Plenum Press.

Yates, F. A. (1966) *The Art of Memory*. Harmondsworth: Pelican, 1978.

Name index

Subject index

ambiguous figures 36
apperception 24, 98–135, 136,
    152–3, 167–8, 176–80
assimilation 25
attention 1, 9, 10, 32–59, 96, 171,
    175–6
attribute (conceptual) 9, 11, 36, 98
arousal 9
automatization 36, 47–9, 150, 175

behaviourism 7, 10, 16–7
best-first search 26
blindfold chess 76–80, 89, 96
bottom-up processing 133
Bristish Museum Algorithm 26

capacity 26, 36–7, 64–9, 77, 90–1,
    96–9, 164–5, 169, 171–6
chaining 125
chess (game) 3, 17–20, 22, 33, 38,
    42, 54–5, 119–20, 174–75, 179
chess-specific relations 85–7
chunking 4, 65–6, 76–80, 85–8, 91,
    173
closing (mental space) 147–50, 162
concept formation 17
conceptual analysis 2, 5, 8–14, 33,
    169
conceptual taboo 14
consciousness 94,
cognitive revolution 1, 2, 10
conditioning 1, 10
conflict resolution 30
connectionism 16

constraint 16
controlled processes 48
content specific 5, 25, 28, 56, 95,
    99, 102–3, 108–35, 139, 167,
    169–70, 177
consciousness 63, 115–16, 134–5

decision-making 17
definition 9–11
detection 42–7
discriminative features 41
Drosophila 3, 4, 11

ELO rating 18–19
embedding 125
empiricism 5
engineering 5
enumeration 42; selective 38; total
    39–40
selective 38
total 39-40
EPAM 86
error 17, 22, 53, 56, 73, 150, 154–8,
    162–5, 170
expectation 16, 25
evaluation 31, 143–7
expertise *see* skill
eye-movements 28, 49–56

figural synthesis 39
fixation 35, 133, 153

Galvanic skin response 159–60
game position 30, 39, 61–2